GORDON MILLS

BORN
TO
RUN

THE DEBBIE
FERGUSON STORY

OXFORD
UNIVERSITY PRESS

OXFORD
UNIVERSITY PRESS

Great Clarendon Street, Oxford, OX2 6DP,
United Kingdom

Oxford University Press is a department of the University of Oxford.
It furthers the University's objective of excellence in research, scholarship,
and education by publishing worldwide. Oxford is a registered trade mark of
Oxford University Press in the UK and in certain other countries

British Library Cataloguing in Publication Data
Data available

978-1-4085-2362-9

1 3 5 7 9 10 8 6 4 2

Printed in China

Acknowledgements

The publishers would like to thank the following for permission to
use their photograph:

Cover: Getty Images

DEDICATION

Debbie would like to dedicate this book to her mother, her godparents, coaches, teachers, Adrian and all Bahamians, black, white, rich or poor, who have a dream. May they realise that without sacrifice, struggle and passion their dreams will remain just dreams. If they have the desire, the dedication and the belief in themselves, they can overcome all obstacles and their dreams can become a reality.

CONTENTS

ACKNOWLEDGEMENTS

I would like to thank all those who willingly allowed me to interview them and gave me so many details of parts of Debbie's life: Sheralyn Anderson, Danielle Bethel, Earla Bethel, Yolanda Burrows, Louise Campbell, George Cleare, Jackie Edwards, Elka Ferguson, Alpheus Finlayson, Savatheda Fynes, Muriel Gibson, Roger Kelty, Andrea Lockhart, Charelle Lockhart, Erma McLeod, Orinthia Nesbeth, Frank 'Pancho' Rahming, Joey Redhead, the late Tommy Robinson, Brent Stubbs and Julie Wilson.

The following gave me support and encouragement, either by listening to me read sections to them or by reading chapters themselves and offering suggestions: Marie Mills, Pamela Moultrie, Patrice Sairsingh and Rob Thomas.

Thanks also to Jamahl Bowe, whose technical expertise and calm reliability meant so much. Finally, I would like to thank Hywel Jones, without whom this book would not have been published.

Gordon Mills

I would like to thank Gordon Mills, who always encouraged me at school and whose door has always been open for me. Without him, this book would not have been possible.

Debbie Ferguson

PROLOGUE

The final of the women's 200 metres at the 2004 Athens Olympics started at 11.20p.m. on 25 August. The crowd in the Olympic Stadium waited expectantly for the last event of the warm, humid night. The Bahamas had one qualifier, drawn in the outside lane, where the runner has no view of her opponents – the least favoured lane of all.

But from the gun it was clear that the Bahamian woman was determined to make a mockery of the lane assignment, as she powered out of the starting blocks and began to devour the track with her familiar long stride. She crossed the line 22.3 seconds later and looked up expectantly at the electronic scoreboard. As the official result was displayed for the world to see, she sank to the track, head down, arms outstretched in a gesture of thanks, relief and satisfaction. She had done it!

The girl who grew up in Bain Town had won a personal, individual medal in an Olympic final. Third place and the bronze medal, to be placed alongside the silver for the relay in Atlanta and the gold for the relay in Sydney. The medal to complete the set: bronze, silver and gold.

She remained prostrate on the tartan as her mind flooded with memories: memories of relatives, friends, mentors, coaches, colleagues; memories of growing up 'Over-the-Hill' in Nassau; memories of her first school sports day, her first inter-school meet, CARIFTA (Caribbean Free Trade Association) Games, NCAA

(National Collegiate Athletic Association) and World Champion-ships, and all the other championships around the globe – people and events that have contributed to the story of Debbie Ferguson, one of the world's premier female athletes, one of the most popular competitors on the circuit, and a Bahamian whose significant place in the nation's sporting story is unquestioned.

CHAPTER 1
THE EARLY YEARS

A talent to nurture

For many people, the story of Debbie Ferguson, triple Olympic medallist, began in 1987 at the Youth CAC meet in Freeport, Grand Bahama, the first time she represented The Bahamas in international competition. She was 11 years old and only a recent addition to the hopeful squad of schoolchildren training at Nassau's Thomas A. Robinson National Stadium.

To fully understand Debbie Ferguson and what contributed to making her who she is, we must go back further, to the summer of 1976, when Debbie and her mother left her native Nassau and flew to her mother's home, Jamaica.

After six months of struggling to make ends meet in Nassau after Debbie's birth, her mother had decided to move back to Jamaica. There she hoped life would be a little easier than it was as a single mother without regular work in Nassau. While being a single mother was not unusual in The Bahamas, bringing up a child without a regular income was proving to be more than she could cope with. She had had to give up her job as a housekeeper when she was seven months pregnant, and there were no other family members nearby. Reluctantly, she had decided to sacrifice her savings to buy a plane ticket and return to Jamaica. There she had family and a support system, where she could live without too many outgoings and provide more easily for her daughter.

Debbie's grandparents were overjoyed at the turn of events and immediately began helping to bring up their granddaughter. They lived in a tiny but comfortable house in Little London, a sprawling town in the parish of Westmoreland that runs along the main A2 road from Savanna la Mar in the south to Negril on the west coast. The settlements in Little London look out onto fields of grassland crossed by meandering rivers. The land is lush and verdant, offering families the opportunity to grow fruit and vegetables. At one time there was abundant sugar cane and the West Indies Sugar Company had a factory in nearby Frome. The industry continues to employ many of Little London's residents, years after the Sugar Company of Jamaica replaced its British-owned predecessor.

While Debbie's grandparents continued to work the land and sell their crops, her mother began to make stiff sweeping brooms from the surrounding vegetation as a way to make money. Debbie flourished under the watchful eyes of her grandparents, both hardworking and determined to live their lives independently, beholden to no one. They both worked the land around the house: Debbie's grandmother grew fruit and vegetables, and her grandfather tended his cattle and cultivated rice in government paddy fields, once worked by transplanted Indian labourers after the demise of slavery.

As the adults worked hard during the long days, Debbie was left in the care of her cousin Beverly, who was just five when the Fergusons arrived. Beverly remembers watching over the baby and nursing her in those early days. She remembers her own astonishment, along with that of the rest of the family, when the tiny newcomer began standing and holding onto chairs at seven months, and actually walking at just nine months.

Westmoreland is one of the smallest parishes in Jamaica and the people are friendly and neighbourly. The parish capital is Savanna

4

la Mar, a busy, concrete jungle of a town where people from the countryside travel daily to do business. There is a restless hustle and bustle about the town, with Great George's Street, the mile-long main thoroughfare, its principal economic hub. At the sea end is the market, teeming with fruit and vegetable traders. Debbie's mother would sometimes come here to sell her brooms. More often, however, she would travel further afield to Kingston, the country's capital, a journey that meant spending the night away in the city. Often she would make few sales and would return tired and disheartened, with very little to show for her efforts. She always came back with some children's clothes, however, either for the baby, or to sell from the wooden shop in front of the house.

Westmoreland natives pride themselves on the fact that they are a very close-knit population and will always provide support for each other. Everyone regards each other as family, so it is little wonder that Debbie's own family were so helpful and encouraging. In Little London there are many small family communities living in separate houses on the same plot of land. The self-contained family units are housed in tiny wooden houses, often sharing a cooking space and an outhouse.

Among the other relatives living close to Debbie's grandparents was her Uncle Forrest. A tall, upright man – something of an entrepreneur in the neighbourhood – Uncle Forrest encouraged his niece to play games of ball and chase, and took her for rides on his motorbike. The bike made him quite a local celebrity and people liked to see him and Debbie speeding around the neighbourhood.

As a small child, therefore, Debbie was the recipient of love, attention and encouragement from her mother, her grandparents and her extended family. These basic elements for successfully raising a child would form the basis of her character. Although there was never very much in a material sense (the family was poor by anyone's standards), Debbie thrived in this loving, affectionate environment. From an early age, both her mother and her grandparents instilled in her high moral standards, alongside the Christian teaching of a belief in God, and the importance of telling the truth and working hard. The family lived by these standards, and as Debbie grew and adopted them more consciously, they became essential parts of her character.

Debbie's grandfather was a humble man, but proud, hardworking and selfless. He was a man of few words, but he contributed to the sense of security Debbie came to feel from the immediate family, and the aunts, uncles and cousins who lived nearby. Debbie's grandfather would tell the young child about his day in the paddy fields, wading through the water, yet feeling the satisfaction that comes from hard physical work. Although life was a constant struggle to survive, the dignity that accompanies honest toil radiated from this man and Debbie responded to the goodness of his soul. Sometimes she would go with him to the rice fields, but was always anxious about the depth of water in the paddies and heeded his warnings about not going into the water. She often accompanied him to feed the cattle, however, riding one of their many donkeys laden with large, grass-filled panniers.

Debbie spent more time with her grandmother, helping to feed the chickens and collect the eggs, milking the goats and picking fruits and vegetables that her grandmother grew in the smallholding. In the late afternoons and evenings, her grandmother would talk to her, read the Bible and tell her Bible stories. This became Debbie's world until she was old enough to go to school.

She remembers one story in particular: the parable of the talents, which had a lasting impact on her as a young child. Debbie would ask her grandmother to tell it to her over and over again, along with her interpretation. Her grandmother gave the parable a modern reading, defining talent as a God-given gift, and Debbie was fascinated by the idea of developing the gift, letting it grow and never neglecting it. Her grandmother would impress on her the importance of using and practising our gifts, not hiding them or simply trying to preserve them. At this time, of course, none of the family had any idea that the five-year-old Debbie had any athletic talent. It is true that she would spend time running around the yard, to the neighbours' houses or to one of the little stores that lined the main road, but no one saw anything unusual in a five-year-old with a lot of energy. She never entered a race and never took part in track competitions while she lived in Jamaica. All that came later, after the move back to The Bahamas.

It is remarkable to think of the global achievements of Jamaican-born athletes on the track since the mid-1970s. Don Quarrie, Merlene Ottey and Veronica Campbell-Brown have won gold medals for their country; many others, such as Linford Christie and Donovan Bailey, have won gold medals for the adopted countries to which their families emigrated. It is a great pity that even now, after such successes, there is insufficient funding to create an infrastructure that allows all the young people in the Jamaican countryside to develop their full potential.

If Debbie had stayed in Westmoreland, it is highly unlikely that her ability would have been nurtured. How many other boys and girls like her have fallen through the cracks and not advanced their talents because the opportunities were not available in rural areas? How many more medals would Jamaica have won in athletic competitions if the infrastructure were in place? We shall never know.

Debbie's cousin, Roy, who was the same age, was her most regular playmate. He recalls: 'I was the fastest runner in the area among the boys, but Debbie could always beat me – in all the games of chase and in the games at school.' By contrast, Debbie remembers many other girls at school who could run faster than she could in games of chase in the school yard. Roy doubts this: his memory is of Debbie outrunning the boys as well as the girls. He adds, however, that there was nothing very organised about the running: it was just small children chasing each other. The idea that there was a future track champion in their midst never entered anyone's head.

Big Bridge Basic

Debbie's first school was about two miles from her grandparents' house in a part of Little London known as Big Bridge. Her first teacher was Ms Erma McLeod, a softly spoken, dedicated educator who served the community of Big Bridge for 33 years as its sole infant-school teacher. When Debbie attended the school, she became part of Ms McLeod's class of more than 50 five- and six-year-olds. In spite of the class size, Ms McLeod remembers her well. 'She was a lovely little girl, always neat and tidy in her sparkling clean white blouse and beautifully pressed red skirt. She made friends easily and she loved to come to school.'

Big Bridge Basic School, with its one inspirational teacher, was Debbie's educational home for two years. In learning terms, 'basic' stands for the fundamentals of learning, but in this case it could easily mean no frills and little equipment. Ms McLeod had a chalkboard, some chalk and little else, but she more than made up for the lack of facilities and equipment by concentrating on three fundamentals of character development: 'I tried to instil in my children the benefits of being loving, caring and honest in all their interactions with other people,' she explains. 'I taught them to respect the truth, and never to lie.'

Ms McLeod recalls one incident involving the young Debbie. 'Her Uncle Forrest would often bring her to school on his motorbike, a 250cc machine that he used to roar around the district on. This particular day he brought her and he was wearing a white shirt and, as he waved goodbye to her, the shirt billowed out in the wind like a ship's sail.

'At the end of school, we were preparing to go home when there was a sudden squeal of brakes, a series of bumps and a clatter from a vehicle on the dirt road outside. A car had spun out of control, hit a tree and the driver had been tossed out as his door flew open on impact. He lay unconscious on the muddy track. When the children and I went out, we saw a car on its side and the driver lying in the road. He was wearing a white shirt, his face down in the mud.

'Debbie was convinced that it was her favourite uncle, still wearing the shirt he had been wearing when he dropped her off that morning. She was beside herself with distress and it was almost impossible to stop her running over to the injured man. I picked her up and hugged her, all the time assuring her that it wasn't Uncle Forrest, that this was a different man altogether. But she was inconsolable. It wasn't until later, when Uncle Forrest arrived on his motorbike, that Debbie began to recover and calm down. Uncle Forrest was able to soothe her and by the time he sat her on the passenger seat, she was smiling again as they made their way home.

'The driver had to be taken to hospital in Savanna la Mar, but eventually he recovered. Yes, Debbie was a very intense little girl: it helped her in her school work, but it sometimes caused her some emotional stress in situations like this.'

9

Ms McLeod has now retired and lives in a small wooden house close to the school she led for all those years. On the walls are a number of plaques in recognition of her years of dedicated teaching at Big Bridge Basic School. Arthritis now prevents her from walking very far, but she happily receives visitors and talks nostalgically and with affection about her years teaching at Big Bridge Basic.

Lassie

Although Debbie had friends of her own age to play with at school, there were no other young girls in the neighbourhood. Debbie cannot remember playing with any friends of her own age other than Roy, but she can remember a puppy that was born when she was five and became her constant companion. The dog was the runt of the litter and had been left behind after people had chosen their puppies. Debbie's sympathy for the underdog had already been cultivated. She named her Lassie after the TV series and made the dog her own. She made a special spot for Lassie with a box and an old blanket, and nursed and fed the undernourished little animal until she grew stronger and more robust.

So began, at the age of five, Debbie's interest in the disenfranchised and underprivileged. It is an interest that has grown and increased as the years have passed, and when she is back in her home town, Debbie is in constant demand to talk to young people in the poorer areas of Nassau and at the Girls' and Boys' Industrial Schools for teenagers at risk. 'I didn't understand what it was at that time,' she explains, 'but I knew I only wanted that one dog and I was actually very pleased when no one else chose her. Since then, I've always found myself drawn to the less privileged or less fortunate, especially children and the elderly. I see children as the future and I see the elderly as always worthy of respect.' Her love of dogs has continued and she currently owns six: Lucky, Speedy, GQ and Scooter live in Nassau with her mother; Paris and Nikki live with Debbie in Miami when she is training. 'They are miniature dogs,' explains Debbie, 'but they are wonderful companions. I love having them because they really brighten up my days.'

Lassie, a mongrel – or potcake, as they are called in the Caribbean – blossomed as a result of Debbie's love and attention. They would run together around the yard, first with the barefoot Debbie chasing the dog, and then the roles would be reversed, with Debbie squealing in delight as the dog chased her. A strong bond developed, so much so that when Debbie switched schools and began attending primary school in Savanna la Mar, Lassie would wait outside in the yard and then, as if by some canine intuition, would start to bark and run around when she sensed that Debbie had arrived on the bus. At first, Debbie's mother and grandmother could not understand what had got into the dog, but all was revealed when Debbie came running along the path from the bus stop.

Her afternoon homecoming marked the restart of their fun and chasing games. This happened every day that Debbie went to school: as if by magic, the dog knew that she had arrived, even though she did not always arrive at the same time. Sometimes Debbie had to catch a later bus as she was unable to get on the first one that came along, having spent her return bus fare on food or sweets during the day. This meant that other children, who had not been so tempted, were allowed on first and, if the bus filled up in the meantime, Debbie had to wait for the next one to come along.

11

Sometimes she did not attend school at all: perhaps she was needed at home, or there was just no money for the bus fare; occasionally, heavy rain would prevent her from making it to the bus stop in time. These were some of the challenges of growing up in rural Jamaica, but she faced them as she has always faced challenges in her life. She hated missing school, because right from the start she loved the classroom, with its interaction with the teachers and other students, and she loved the freedom of running and playing in the big recreational yard outside. She did quite well there, supported by her mother and grandparents, who taught her how important it was to be disciplined.

Even as a young girl, Debbie was always encouraged to come home and do her reading and her homework before she was allowed to go outside to play. This disciplined approach to life was to play a vital part in her academic and sporting successes later on, both at secondary school and at college. It was while she was living with her grandparents that this lesson, repeated by her mother and her grandparents, was etched in her mind, from where it has never been erased.

Around this time, the family was shaken by the news that cousin Bev, who was now 14 and had recently met a boy from a nearby settlement, had fallen pregnant. The news was unexpected, but not particularly surprising: teenage pregnancy accounts for over 50 per cent of births in Caribbean countries. It is seen by many as ironic that there are so many teenage pregnancies among people with such deep respect for the teachings of the church and who try to follow a Christian way of life whenever they can. Debbie's grandparents, however, took the news in their stride, telling Debbie that soon she would have a new playmate. Debbie looked forward to the new arrival.

Return to Nassau

When Debbie was nine, her mother began to feel frustrated with her life in Westmoreland. Money was still scarce and the various enterprises she had tried to start up had not developed as she had hoped. She wanted more for herself and hankered after the kind of life she had once led in Nassau. She felt that, given a fair chance, she could do quite well back in The Bahamas. She was also becoming disappointed with Debbie's schooling, as she could see her daughter's potential, recognising that Debbie was a good, enthusiastic student who loved school and was doing very well, but was limited by a lack of extracurricular opportunities. She was also concerned at the school days Debbie was forced to miss through no fault of her own.

In Nassau, they could live within walking distance of a school and Debbie would never have to miss a day. The flourishing tourist industry in The Bahamas meant that it was possible to earn more money there than in rural Jamaica. Debbie's mother thought that there was a better infrastructure in Nassau, with more opportunities for a young child, so after much soul searching she made the decision to go back to The Bahamas. Although her parents tried to persuade her not to go, warning her that she would again be alone with her child and would have no one to assist her, Debbie's mother was determined to go back.

This was to prove the most important decision that influenced Debbie's life: without it, there would have been no athletics career, no university education and no place on the world's sporting stage.

Debbie really did not know what to think about this move; she hated the idea of being separated from all her family and close friends in Little London, but she was excited by the opportunity of going to school regularly and by the idea of returning to her home in another country. Nevertheless, it would mean giving up so much: Lassie, her constant companion when she was at home; her grandparents, who meant so much to her; Bev and the baby that was soon to arrive; Roy and Uncle Forrest; and the freedom of the open spaces around the house. Still only a child, she could not be expected to see the benefits of a school nearby, regular work for her mother or a variety of stores just a short distance away – not to mention the possibility of friendships with children who lived close by and attended the same school.

On more than one occasion, when the topic of the move was mentioned, Debbie would give vent to what she describes as her 'famous temper'. This temper hardly ever reveals itself now, but there were times when she was young that it led to tantrums as she tried to get her own way. Debbie soon realised, however, that nothing was going to change by her becoming angry, and gradually she disciplined herself to control these outbursts. She still feels the same anger from time to time, but she covers it up very successfully: in fact, if you ask anyone who knows Debbie about her 'bad temper' or 'tantrums', or even moods, they look at you as if you are talking about someone else! Those characteristics are now quite alien to her.

As her mother made preparations for the move and it became ever more certain, Debbie accepted it stoically, while seeking comfort in the warmth and understanding of her grandparents. They were obviously going to miss their granddaughter, whose presence did so much to brighten their days, but they recognised the reasons behind her mother's decision and always spoke positively to Debbie about it. The phrase 'God's will' was often used to explain it, and slowly Debbie came to accept the influence of a higher being. In spite all this, however, Debbie nearly did not make the trip.

In the yard of her mother's house were trees that Debbie loved to climb, including one that had branches hanging over the small hut from which her mother sold the clothes she brought back from Kingston. The hut was actually on the other side of the fence and close to the road. It had a dangerous, steeply sloping roof. Debbie had always been told she must not climb on the roof and she resisted the temptation, knowing that she would receive a spanking if she set foot on its uneven surface, but one day the temptation became too much. From her precarious position on the overhanging branch, she gingerly stepped onto the galvanised zinc, little realising that not only was it sloping steeply, but burning hot in the midday sun. Barefoot, she was forced to make a quick move to relieve the pain. She lost her balance and slid and slipped, bumping her bottom on the scorching surface until there was no more roof and she fell the eight feet to the dusty ground below. She landed on her bottom in the dust and quickly looked around to see if anyone had observed her hasty descent from the forbidden rooftop: no one was there.

She was just dusting herself off, checking her legs and feet for scratches and preparing to find Lassie for a game of chase, when her mother came out of the house. She saw Debbie dusting herself down in front of the shed, put two and two together and marched over to chastise her. Debbie remembers that the pain she felt on her bottom from the fall was definitely augmented by the punishment for disobedience and doing such a dangerous thing. Luckily, she suffered no lasting damage, the pain quickly wore off and the only thing left hurt was her nine-year-old pride. The incident served as a salutary lesson that when adults make rules for children there is usually a good reason. Debbie rarely questioned her mother's rules after this, and managed to resist most temptations. There was no permanent injury, but Debbie definitely did not go near that tree, or the shed, for the rest of the time that she remained in Jamaica.

Looking back, Debbie realises that she could have suffered a serious injury, and who knows what could have been the effect of such an injury on her life? The running talent might have been extinguished before it had had a chance to manifest itself; the opportunities that that talent put in her path would never have appeared and her glittering track career might never have begun.

During the next few months, Debbie's mother made plans and arrangements for their return to Nassau. Debbie was now resigned to the move, but still could not come to terms with all that it was going to mean. Her mother told her about the house they were going to move into with an adopted aunt named Doralee. Aunt Doralee had four children and lived on a street with lots of other houses nearby, so there would be many other children to play with. Aunt Doralee had registered Debbie at Oakes Field Primary School, where she could start as soon as they arrived in Nassau. Debbie continued to have long talks with her grandmother about going to live in The Bahamas, and continued to receive encouragement from her. Her grandmother explained that the move represented a great opportunity to discover and develop the many special talents she had. Eventually, Debbie began to believe this selfless and inspiring advice and actually started to look forward to moving. She knew she was going to miss so many things about Jamaica – after all, it was the only home she had ever really known – but, young as she was, she understood that it was a chance to better herself and was already determined not to miss any opportunity to fulfil her potential and broaden her possibilities in life.

Just a few months before Debbie and her mother were due to depart, cousin Bev gave birth to a baby girl. When mother and baby came home from the maternity ward, Debbie was mesmerised by the helpless little being and constantly asked if she could nurse her. For a short while, baby Stacie would replace Lassie as the object of Debbie's affections, but with her 10-year-old's energy level and love of running and chasing with the dog, she would always return to Lassie and their games of chase in the yard.

One day, when Stacie was three months old and Debbie was nursing her, she became fretful and would not respond to Debbie's cuddles. She had observed this type of behaviour before and had watched Bev calm her by feeding her. Debbie reasoned that it was food she needed. She lifted the baby, went to the kitchen area and found some cheese which she began to cut up into small pieces. Having put the cheese on a small plate, she returned to the small sitting room and began to try to feed the cheese to the baby.

Three-month-old babies are not familiar with cheese, of course, nor any solid food for that matter, and Stacie's crying did not diminish; in fact, it grew stronger. Debbie continued to try to push the cheese into the baby's mouth, to no avail. She was beginning to become more and more frustrated when Bev walked in from collecting eggs in the field. Bev was horrified to see her baby with cheese all over her face, but quickly realised that Debbie was only acting out of love and concern. She could not be angry; she could not even scold her, but simply took the baby in her arms, found a bottle and told Debbie that cheese was for grown-ups and that babies need to drink from bottles.

'She was doing what she thought was best for the baby,' says Bev, 'but it could have been dangerous. I told Debbie babies do not take solid food like cheese until they are older and I explained how it could choke them if it stuck in their throats. She felt so bad about what she had done. "I didn't mean it, I didn't mean it," she cried and was very upset that she might have harmed baby Stacie.'

The day to leave the familiar surroundings of Westmoreland finally came and Debbie said her tearful goodbyes to the family she loved: her grandparents, cousin Bev and baby Stacie, Uncle

Forrest and cousin Roy, and reserved the longest and biggest hug for Lassie, her partner in the games of chase.

Debbie and her mother soon found themselves speeding along the climbing, twisting road, passing Big Bridge and Bramble, the enormous dairy farm at Montpelier, across the Great River, and eventually over the mountains and down to Sangster International Airport at Montego Bay. They checked in, made their way to the departure lounge and at long last onto the Air Jamaica flight to Nassau.

Although this was not the first time that Debbie had been on a plane, she had no recollection of the first flight, as she was only a few months old at the time. She thoroughly enjoyed the trip, watching the television screen, looking out of the window, making the seat recline and enjoying the soft drinks served by the cabin crew. All too quickly the flight ended and the plane taxied to the ramp at Nassau International Airport. Debbie and her mother had touched down on Bahamian soil again.

And so began the next phase of Debbie's life, the phase that changed her life forever and set her on the path to success, fame and personal fulfilment.

CHAPTER 2
EARLY SCHOOLDAYS IN NASSAU

On the move

On their return to Nassau, Debbie and her mother went to live in a small house in Baldwin Avenue, Chippingham, about a mile from downtown Nassau (and, coincidentally, just a stone's throw from the Queen Elizabeth Sports Centre and the Thomas A. Robinson National Stadium). Chippingham was an area of tight-knit, working-class black Bahamians striving to improve their lives. It was very much part of what had come to be called by the locals 'Over-the-Hill', referring to the hill that separates the commercial centre of Bay Street from the poorer areas inland. The house was small, with two bedrooms, and the Fergusons shared it with Doralee, Debbie's mother's adopted sister, and her four children. It was quite a squeeze: Debbie shared one of the bedrooms with her mother, and there were few comforts. Running water was not available; Debbie had to use the pump in the yard, and hot water came via a pot on the stove.

The ready-made friends close to her own age helped to take Debbie's mind off all the family members left behind in Jamaica and the outdoor life she used to lead with Lassie. Ms Ferguson remembers Debbie making the adjustment very easily, and Debbie herself does not remember allowing feelings of homesickness for her grandparents and the surroundings of Westmoreland to upset her. Rather, she can remember playing chase, stick ball and climbing trees with Aunt Doralee's children, Tony, Fonce, Kevin and Pammy, and the next-door neighbours, the Chipmans. All games, however, had to take place after school work was finished, just as in Jamaica. Debbie's mother was strict and consistent in applying the rule that the first thing to do when she arrived home from Oakes Field Primary School was her homework. Debbie never questioned this. She knew that one of the main reasons they had come to Nassau was for her to attend school every day and receive a more regular education, so she was determined not to let this opportunity slip through her fingers. Ms Ferguson often repeated to Debbie that, after God, education was the most important thing. She told her daughter that she must not waste it. Debbie took her words to heart: even at the age of 10, she did not want to let down either her mother or her grandparents, who had all persuaded her that the educational possibilities in Nassau made it worth leaving Westmoreland.

Church and school were the dominant factors in the young Debbie's life. Ms Ferguson wanted to set her daughter on the 'right path', as she called it. They attended church regularly on Sunday mornings, Sunday nights, Monday nights and Wednesday nights. On the other evenings, Ms Ferguson let Debbie watch television with the other children in the house after her school work was finished, but only until 8p.m., when she had to go to bed. 'A growing girl needs her rest', she would tell her daughter. 'Your mind needs to rebuild itself through the night, ready for the next day's learning.'

Apart from her school books, Debbie had very little to call her own in those early days back in Nassau. She would often look on as other girls played with fancy dolls that cried, walked or wet themselves, and wondered why she had none of her own. She knew that a certain doll was pretty or had beautiful clothes, and often wished that she had one too, but her mother had taught her not to covet these things and to be satisfied with what she had, no matter how little it might be. When she did, rarely, receive a doll, she would shower it with affection and, like most little girls, copy the way her mother had spoken to her. She would call the doll Stacie, remembering the times she had nursed cousin Bev's baby, and whisper to it just as she had to Stacie.

Although their involvement at church provided spiritual stability for Debbie, the family living arrangements were anything but stable. The cramped conditions at Doralee's led them to move to another place in Chippingham, and from there they moved again, to Bain Town. Very soon after that they changed dwellings once more, this time to a little house in Grant's Town: three moves in little more than a year. Debbie was not unsettled by all the changes: 'Each time it seemed there was a little improvement,' she says positively. 'They were all tiny and none had inside bathrooms or running water, but by the time we moved to Grant's Town, Mom and I had our own rooms and a small sitting room. It wasn't comfortable by some standards. It was still in what Nassau people regard as a ghetto area, but we were okay there. We actually stayed there for about eight years. The neighbours were very friendly and helpful and shared a lot with us.'

A father figure?

One person who was not there to share very much with Debbie during the first 10 years of her life was her father. Debbie's mother had not been married to her father, and Debbie did not even know him. She was only a few months old when she and her mother left Nassau and there had been no contact with him since. Debbie can remember no mention of him by her mother or her grandparents during all the time they were in Jamaica. When they returned to Nassau, however, Debbie's mother thought it would be a good idea for Debbie to try to establish a relationship with her father. He was a prison officer at Nassau's Fox Hill Prison and lived a mere five minutes from the Fergusons, in the same Oakes Field neighbourhood.

So Debbie started to visit the man whom she was encouraged to call Daddy, but to whom she was never able to give that name. The atmosphere was stiff and unnatural, made all the worse by the fact that Debbie's mother rarely came with her. Debbie felt uncomfortable and her father seemed incapable of breaking the ice or treating her affectionately. Only one visit is fixed in Debbie's memory and that remains there for all the wrong reasons.

One day, after school, her mother told her it was time to go and visit her father again. Debbie complained because she did not want to spend another boring few hours feeling uncomfortable with a man she hardly knew, but her mother insisted, still hoping that Debbie would forge a relationship with the man. 'You should want to get to know your own daddy,' she said.

In the event, the visit had had serious consequences. Debbie's father became angry at her refusal to show him the affection she did not feel. When she fell and hurt her head, her father just remained in his armchair, shocked, while Debbie managed to pick up the homework she had been trying to do and ran home as fast as she could to Baldwin Avenue. She told her bewildered mother exactly what had happened. Ms Ferguson felt the back of Debbie's head, with its lump already developing, and told her to hurry and pump some water and put it on the stove to boil.

'That is all I can remember,' recalls Debbie, 'because I started to feel dizzy, and before I knew what was going on, I passed out right in front of the stove. They had to rush me to the hospital because they couldn't get me to wake up.' Extremely anxious, and feeling guilty for having caused this unfortunate chain of events, Ms Ferguson was hugely relieved when Debbie woke up in the ambulance. 'By this time there was an enormous bump on my head and, as you would expect with a head injury, the doctors insisted on a battery of tests and X-rays. Fortunately, nothing showed up and pretty soon I was feeling much better and they let me go home.'

That was the last time she ever went to her father's house and her mother stopped urging her to see him. Debbie reckons that she has only seen him about half a dozen times since that day. Despite her successes and achievements, he has never shown any inclination to make contact with her and, after this incident, she certainly did not want to see him. 'It's funny how things that happen long ago have a habit of playing a part in our lives much later,' muses Debbie: this blow to the head had significant repercussions later, when she was at the University of Georgia, but for the time being, she felt well and there were no after-effects.

Potential spotted

Having taken the place at Oakes Field Primary School for which she had been registered, Debbie entered Grade 5 determined to excel. She did well in all subjects and impressed her teachers with her positive, determined and friendly attitude, and her polite manner. Only one surprising part of school life proved difficult at first: mixing with other children. For one so gregarious and naturally friendly, this seems incongruous, but Debbie was self-conscious about her Jamaican accent and the patois that she spoke. She hated hearing the other children ask her, 'Why you speak so funny?' To avoid the mocking questions, such as 'Why don't you go back to Jamaica?'

and 'You a rasta, hey?' Debbie decided not to speak very much at all. Her mother recalls that she was naturally quiet at this time anyway, so she was quite comfortable with her self-imposed silence.

Secretly, Debbie practised speaking in a way that erased all traces of her Jamaican accent. She was still young enough for it to have happened naturally, but as if she knew losing the accent would take too long, she practised speaking English with a Bahamian accent at home in the evenings to speed up the process. Soon she began to sound like her classmates: gradually the questions and hurtful remarks dwindled, until eventually they stopped and she found herself accepted completely.

Two other factors were very important for Debbie in establishing her own place in the social structure of the classroom, and both contributed to her being accepted by the other children in the class. One was the outstanding standard of her school work, and the other, of course, was her athletic and sporting talent. This became apparent as soon as she stepped onto the field in a sports lesson. Sporting talent was, as it still is, a definite factor in gaining respect from one's peers.

Andrea Lockhart, the sports teacher at Oakes Field Primary and one of the biggest influences on Debbie's life, spotted her talents immediately. She was surprised, however, to hear from her that she had never run a competitive race before and had not been in any sort of after-school track programme. She could see that Debbie had the makings of a successful athlete and encouraged her to go to Frank 'Pancho' Rahming's evening track and field programme at the Queen Elizabeth Sports Centre. Here her talent could be nurtured. 'I wanted her to go to someone I could trust,' says Lockhart. 'So many coaches push young children too hard and cause irreparable damage to young limbs and bodies. I knew Pancho would treat her well. Even then I was thinking of her future. Track and field can be the ticket to scholarships at university, and if she did well and represented The Bahamas, she might be offered the chance of a university education. I didn't want this talent to go to waste when she left us. I would have worked with her for two years before she moved on and I didn't want her to go to just any track club. I wanted her to go to one that would get the best out of her in the best way.'

Even though she was winning races in sports lessons, Debbie was surprised when her teacher made this suggestion. She knew her mother would look unfavourably on any activity that took her away from her study time in the evenings, because she knew that Ms Ferguson did not want anything to interfere with her education.

Her mother's words would ring in her ears: 'When you goes to school, you don't follow other children, you goes to learn. Look at the kind of work I does. You wants to do better than that – domestic work, washing and cleaning for other people. One of the family has got to come to be someone. When you in lessons and something troubling you that you don't understand, you have a hand, you hold it up and the teacher will recognise that you need help. And before you go to play, you ask the teacher to give you extra help. I tell you, education is the key.'

Debbie knew that her mother believed this firmly and wanted Debbie to believe it too. She knew that persuading her mother to agree to track practices after school was not going to be easy. As well as the important school work, there was regular attendance at church to consider. To convince her mother that training after school was a positive addition to these activities was going to take all of the 10-year-old's powers of persuasion. In fact, Debbie did not even want to broach the subject with her mother, so asked Ms Lockhart if she would do it for her. Ms Lockhart agreed, because she wanted her new pupil, with her exciting potential, to have every chance to develop what she saw as a special talent.

The meeting was not quite the obstacle that Debbie imagined it was going to be. Her mother was impressed by Ms Lockhart's sincerity and concern, and was quite willing to give her consent – at first. Of course, she impressed upon Debbie the need to keep up with her work and told her firmly that if there was ever a drop in her grades, or if the programme ever caused her to miss homework, then she would have to give up the running. To Debbie, this seemed fair enough.

At this time, she had no idea just how much running would come to mean to her; nor did she know how much time was going to be involved. On many occasions after Debbie had come home late from an extended practice, her mother told her it would all have to stop because it was taking up too much time. Debbie would tell Ms Lockhart what her mother had said; the sports teacher knew that she would have to visit Ms Ferguson again to persuade her to allow Debbie to continue with the training. In this way, Ms Lockhart became closely involved with Debbie and her mother. Ms Ferguson came to rely on the sports teacher's assistance to keep Debbie focused on her studies. Ms Lockhart also became aware of Ms Ferguson's difficulties supporting herself and her daughter. She arranged two babysitting jobs that brought in some much-needed revenue. Later, she provided more help by purchasing a freezer for them so that Ms Ferguson could sell cups of frozen juice from her front porch to add to the candies and cookies.

'Debbie's approach to life inspired me to do all I could for them,' states Lockhart, 'and I gladly helped them in any way I could. To see her striving so hard at school and doing so well made me want to try all the more to improve things for her at home.'

Needless to say, Debbie always kept her side of the bargain and completed her school work on time and to an excellent standard, even though it often meant she had to stay up well past the normal bedtime for one of her age.

The relationship between Debbie and Andrea Lockhart soon developed into something much more than pupil and sports teacher. Responding to Ms Lockhart's interest and desire to do what was best for her, Debbie grew close to her teacher and was invited to the family house for weekends. This was a natural extension of Lockhart's role as liaison between school, track and home. Ms Ferguson gave her blessing for Debbie to spend time with Ms Lockhart and her two sons, Thackeray and Labosky. The two boys, younger than Debbie, grew very fond of her. She loved staying with them all, mothering the boys and playing their video games. The boys took it in turns to give up their rooms for her when she came, and never complained!

A coach appears

Debbie attended Pancho Rahming's junior training sessions after school. Her routine became one of school interspersed with training: washing and ironing school uniform in the morning before leaving for the track, training in the mornings before school, training again after school, and homework when she arrived home. The self-discipline needed to maintain this lifestyle gave her the impetus to keep going and had a positive impact on her life. As she explained, 'Other girls had ballet or piano lessons for their hobbies. I had track and that was my ballet or piano.'

Pancho Rahming is quietly spoken, with an acute eye for his sprinters' well-being and development. He urges rather than commands, and he gets to know his athletes in a personal and meaningful way. Debbie, seeing some similarities between Rahming and her grandfather, loved him from the start, listened to him as intently as she could, would never hear a bad word said about him, and tried to do everything as he instructed. He became her surrogate father and she listened to every word of his advice; she even called him 'Daddy'.

At the track in the afternoons Debbie made a huge impression. Her enthusiasm was infectious and Rahming remembers how, from the first session she attended, she impressed not only him but many of the older athletes. She was very willing and determined. Many of the older girls were inspired by the new girl to come out and train harder. Debbie never seemed tired, never refused to complete a drill and never showed any reluctance to take part in any activities. She always pushed herself to the limit.

For children of Debbie's age there was little specialisation during these training sessions. She was expected to sprint, run longer distances, jump and throw, even though speed work revealed her true ability. Rahming remembers that she happily worked at both high jump and long jump, excelling in both through her natural speed.

Wherever they trained – the beach, the track, Fort Charlotte with its grassy hills – Debbie loved it and ran as if her life depended on it. She loved running from the start. It was no infatuation or long courtship, getting to know each other and falling out from time to time. This was her real true love, so much so that she wondered how she had survived for so long without it!

Rahming still remembers the first evening that Ms Lockhart brought Debbie to the track and introduced her. He was struck by her manners and her 10-year-old self-confidence. Debbie cannot explain the apparent self-confidence because she actually felt quite nervous meeting a real coach at a real track. She had never seen anywhere like the stadium before – all her previous running had been on patchy grass. The track, with its eight painted lanes and springy tartan surface, filled her with awe and she felt excited, but nervous. The manners, however, are easier to explain. Her mother had always impressed upon her the importance of politeness. 'Good manners will get you anywhere,' she would tell her daughter, a lesson echoed by her grandmother. 'Yes, please. No, thank you. Yes, sir. Yes, ma'am. These can be your passport to the stars. They will take you anywhere,' her mother would say. Debbie responded until these things were as natural as breathing. They remain so today.

When Pancho Rahming set Debbie off to run around the track on that first evening, her style and running technique impressed him immediately. Never one to resort to exaggeration, or even too much enthusiasm before he has made a full assessment, Rahming was, in spite of himself, very excited by what he saw. For one so young, who had never been coached before, Debbie's first session at the track was remarkable. Her stride was long and rhythmic, her body type compact and explosive. Rahming recognised that here was a girl whose potential looked very promising indeed. She did not have tremendous leg speed, but had natural leg strength: she covered the ground quickly because of a natural explosion in her stride. (Rahming actually believes that Debbie has always needed more leg speed to be a true contender for 100-metre honours. He feels sure that the 200 metres or even the 400 metres is her best event.)

Rahming spoke quietly and sincerely to Ms Lockhart as Debbie went through her paces on the track. He could not believe that she had never been coached and was shocked that she had never even run a competitive race. He asked Ms Lockhart questions about Debbie's family and her home situation and how often she would be able come to the track. Ms Lockhart told him as much as she knew and added that she would often be able to bring Debbie to the track, but not always. Fortunately, the school was not very far from the stadium. When Ms Lockhart had other commitments, Debbie was able to make her own way there – usually at a sprint along the streets – without any problems.

Rahming's real concern was how committed Debbie would be allowed to be. Ms Lockhart had told him how Debbie was well aware of her mother's absolute insistence that school work must take priority. Rahming did not foresee any problems with this, although he was aware that tiring sessions on the track after a long day at school would take their toll on a young girl's body from time to time. In fact, he supported Ms Ferguson's stance and has always wanted his athletes to maintain their focus on their studies and to prioritise their commitments carefully so that they can, if possible, attain the best of both worlds. So he knew that with Debbie they would have to walk the delicate tightrope of school work and training very carefully, but his years of experience told him they could do it.

Even though Rahming is not a 'screamer', he is a hard taskmaster who demands a lot from his charges. He sets them attainable goals, but goals that they will have to push themselves to achieve. His positive attitude also inspires confidence in his protégés. When Debbie first went to him there were two other outstanding girls working with him: Sugar Smith and Jackie Edwards. Unfortunately, Sugar Smith never realised her full potential, but at that time she could hold her own with Debbie and would often beat her. Jackie Edwards is a world-class long jumper who has often represented The Bahamas in the Olympic Games, World Championships and other international competitions.

At that time, the two other girls were inspired by Debbie's intensity and enjoyment, right to the last set of exercises or the final step of the sprint. This talent and ability to encourage other athletes still exists today and serves to encourage all aspiring athletes, be they Olympians or simply honest club runners. When back in Nassau, Debbie will often find herself at the track in the late afternoon, passing on words of encouragement and tips for improvement to youngsters just starting on the long road to athletic stardom. She remembers how she felt as a 10-year-old and always sincerely aims to motivate Rahming's young hopefuls. She knows from personal experience how the track can open many doors to eventual professional fulfilment. She also remembers Ms Lockhart's words and her desire that her charges reach their full potential in all areas so they can take advantage of scholarship opportunities later in life.

As the weeks passed, Debbie became Rahming's personal athlete. He readily communicated with Ms Lockhart so she knew exactly what was happening. Lockhart would follow up on some aspects of the training and could also lend a hand if there were any problems. She was adept at helping Debbie to come to terms with minor emotional difficulties. As was only natural, Debbie would occasionally feel homesick for her grandparents and their smallholding in Westmoreland, and tearful at the prospect of never seeing them again.

Ms Lockhart reassured Debbie: 'The same sun that rises on your grandparents in Jamaica rises on you here in Nassau. One day soon you will see them and you can tell them about all the wonderful things you are doing at school in The Bahamas.' Debbie knew her grandparents and all the other relatives in Little London were supporting her and praying for to succeed in Nassau. They wanted only the best for her. Debbie did not want to let them down by not achieving her potential.

Grades 5 and 6

At school Debbie was achieving great things. Her Grade 5 teacher, Muriel Gibson, remembers how she arrived completely focused on her school work and never lost that focus. She strove for perfection in everything she did. This characteristic really surprised Ms Gibson: she had never seen it manifested quite so strongly in a 10-year-old.

One day, Debbie made a mistake in a maths exercise which resulted in her scoring 19 out of 20. When the class was dismissed for lunch, Ms Gibson found the mortified Debbie in tears.

'Debbie, what are you crying for?' asked the concerned teacher.

'I got one of the sums wrong.'

'Well, Debbie, you're bound to make a mistake from time to time,' reasoned Ms Gibson. 'Make the correction and all will be well.'

But Debbie did not see it like that and she continued to cry all through the break. Ms Gibson comforted her and eventually, as much as she hated having to make the correction, Debbie put the matter right. In her young mind she vowed that she would never have to do a correction again. Ms Gibson cannot remember her making any more errors in maths for the rest of the year. So determined was she to maintain her 100 per cent record that she rarely went out to play during the breaks, preferring to stay in the classroom, reading her books and learning her lessons.

As soon as she arrived in Oakes Field Primary School, Debbie was at the top of her class and never moved from that position. She resisted distractions whenever school work had to be done and sustained her focus throughout the year. It was as if the track practices inspired her to excel at school as well. She knew that continuing to attend the track depended on her ability to keep on top of the school work, so she never let the schoolwork slip and, more importantly, she never let the standard slip either.

The quest for perfection manifested itself in another way too. Children in Grade 5 at Oakes Field were allowed to use erasers to rub out any errors, and they all took advantage of this to make their work look flawless. Debbie had other ideas. She refused to use an eraser, believing that it made things too easy. She wanted to get every piece of work right from the very beginning, the first time round. She did not want messy smudge marks to spoil her work. Ms Gibson impressed upon her that the school allowed its pupils in Grade 5 to use erasers, but Debbie was adamant and never used one.

After Debbie had been at the school for three months, her class was scheduled to take the school assembly in celebration of Thanksgiving. Ms Gibson rehearsed them in a short play about the first settlers in the United States and every child had a part. Debbie had a speech to say. She was still a little self-conscious about her accent. So she practised and practised to pronounce the words as perfectly as she could. Nobody was going to be able to detect any trace of a Jamaican accent if Debbie Ferguson had anything to do with it! In fact, she practised rather too much because when the moment came for her to speak her line, she announced in her finest Queen's English, 'The thurkey has been stolen,' much to the amusement of many in the audience. Ms Gibson remembers that there was plenty of good-natured teasing after this little mistake!

During her first year at Oakes Field, Debbie took part in her first inter-school track meet, representing her school against other primary schools in Nassau. Ms Lockhart selected her for a number of short sprints, the high jump and the long jump: Debbie won them all. All the teachers at Oakes Field, from the principal down, were now very much aware that here was a very special girl. She was maintaining an 'A' average, could outrun all the other girls in her age group in Nassau, and was also a model of politeness and good manners.

As far as sports were concerned, it was not only on the track that Debbie excelled. She was the pitcher on Ms Lockhart's softball team and the captain of the volleyball team too. It seemed there was nothing that she could not do and did not do well. Lockhart remembers Debbie's sporting prowess at Oakes Field: 'She was just outstanding in all sports.' The next year she continued in much the same way, taking to Grade 6 as readily as she had taken to Grade 5. She had a different teacher, of course, Ms Cheralyn Anderson, with whom she quickly established a positive rapport. Debbie valued everything Ms Anderson said to her and wanted to please her from the very first day.

Trying to do what Ms Anderson told her to the last detail, however, almost caused a problem during the first two weeks of Grade 6. Although the pupils in Grade 5 had been allowed to use erasers, Ms Anderson would not allow them to continue with the practice in Grade 6. 'I wanted them to take enough care that they would not need to rub out mistakes,' she explains, 'but I did give them a two-week grace period at the beginning of the year when they could use them to "get erasers out of their systems", as I put it.' Debbie, who had never used an eraser in Grade 5, must have misunderstood her new teacher because she came in the next morning with her eyes puffy and red. Ms Anderson asked her what the problem was and if she had done her homework. Debbie replied that she had done the homework, so Ms Anderson asked again, 'What's the problem then? Why are you crying?' This time Debbie told her through her tears, 'I told my mommy you said we should use an eraser for these two weeks and she wanted me to use the eraser but I couldn't use it.'

Ms Anderson was puzzled, but all was revealed minutes later when Ms Ferguson arrived at the classroom. 'Ms Anderson,' she said, 'I don't know what you did to my daughter. I just could not get her to use an eraser. She made a mistake but I just could not get her to use an eraser.' Ms Anderson quickly saw the misunderstanding and explained it to them. 'You don't have to use an eraser.' She explained, 'In fact, I don't want you to use one. But for these two weeks students can rub out mistakes until they are used to working without one. Debbie and her mother understood the mistake Debbie had made and, when she realised she should not be using an eraser, Debbie cheered up immediately.

From then on, she and her teacher got on so well together that Debbie regularly skipped break time to stay and talk with her, just as she had done the previous year with Ms Gibson. Ms Anderson would often take Debbie home with her at the weekends. She had a daughter of Debbie's age, Nadia, whom she hoped would feel the influence of Debbie's motivation, determination and focus. The two girls got on very well together and Debbie enjoyed the time she spent at the Andersons' house.

Ms Anderson became another chauffeur for track practices and began to play an increasing part in Debbie's development, both academic and sporting. She often found herself, together with Ms Lockhart, listening to her star pupil's worries and concerns, not only during the school day, but also at weekends. Most of Debbie's questions involved her immediate future, moving from primary to secondary school, and what it would be like with all those older boys and girls, and all the others of her own age moving from the other primary schools in the area.

Both Anderson and Lockhart impressed upon Debbie that she need not worry because she had all the necessary attributes to succeed. There was absolutely no reason that she should not go on in the same way at secondary school. They also reminded her that her new school, C.C. Sweeting Junior High School, was only a little way along the street and that former Oakes Field pupils were always returning to see their old teachers after school. They encouraged Debbie to do the same, not only if something was

35

troubling her, but also just to tell them how she was getting on. Debbie never forgot this invitation and went to see her teachers at Oakes Field whenever she could. She would tell them about her days at C.C. and they, true to their word, were always more than pleased to see her.

Throughout her Grade 6 year, Debbie lit up Oakes Field Primary School academically, maintaining an unblemished record in all her subjects. She continued to shine in the sporting arena as well, winning all her races in the inter-house sports, crushing the opposition from other schools in the inter-school meets, and striking out batters with her fast pitches. But the highlight of her Grade 6 year, her first full year of serious track and field, was selection for The Bahamas team to go to the Youth Central America and Caribbean Games in Freeport, Grand Bahama. Her mother remembers her coming home excitedly one evening from practice at the stadium, rushing through the door and announcing, 'Mommy, Mommy, I made the team!'

'What kind of team you made?'

'Mommy, Mommy, I can run.'

'You sure you can run?'

'Yes, I'm on the team, because I can run.' Ms Ferguson thought about this, unsure what to say or what to think. Eventually, she sat Debbie down and said, 'I'm not really interested in running – I more interested in the schooling.'

'But Mommy, I'm in the team. I'm running for The Bahamas,' shouted Debbie, and these words caused Ms Ferguson to stop short. She suddenly realised that her daughter's evenings at the track had some real meaning. She was going to run for The Bahamas against other countries in the region. 'My Debbie must have some real talent,' she thought.

It took another visit from Ms Lockhart to convince Ms Ferguson completely that she should allow Debbie to join the team, but she consented to let Debbie go, adding as usual that she must balance the school work with the training. 'If your grades drop, there'll be no more running,' she added. But although the meaning was clear, this time it was without the earlier threatening tone.

The Bahamas Youth CAC team represented the country in the CAC Games to be held in Freeport. These games are based on the heptathlon and are designed to allow individual athletes to show their talents in different disciplines. Debbie had to run the 60 metres, 200 metres and 800 metres, compete in the long jump and the high jump, and throw the softball.

There was, however, one significant problem: footwear. Anxious for Debbie to perform as well as she possibly could, Coach Rahming had advised her to buy some spiked running shoes, or sprints, as Bahamians call them. When Debbie asked her mother about the possibility of buying a pair, Ms Ferguson exclaimed, 'Where you think I gonna find that kind of money? It took all I could find to get those little tennis you been using.'

'But Mr Rahming says I can do better if I wear sprints.'

'Then maybe Mr Rahming can buy them,' retorted Ms Ferguson, and Debbie, crestfallen, had to leave it at that.

Nonetheless, Debbie did have a new pair of sprints to wear in Freeport for the CAC Games. They came not from Coach Rahming, but from an unsurprising source. Ms Lockhart recounts, 'As soon as Debbie told me what her mother had said about the sprints, I decided to buy them for her. It was the least I could do. I wanted her to do her best in Freeport. She was so proud of them that she did not want to wear them in case they got dusty. She would wipe them clean and kept them in the polythene bag they came in for a very long time.'

New sprints or not, the CAC Championships were quite a challenge. But Debbie exuded confidence from the outset and seemed quite unconcerned by the importance of the event. Her confidence was justified too, because at the end of the meet, she was overall champion. Her first international competition and she had won it!

Returning to school, she found that the topic of conversation soon came to be dominated by one thing: the imminent departure of the Grade 6 students to take their places in secondary school.

The principal of Oakes Field wanted the best for her outstanding student. She encouraged Debbie to take the entrance examination for the Anglican Education Authority schools. They had two secondary schools in Nassau, both private and fee-paying. Debbie took the exam one Saturday morning with a number of other Grade 6 pupils from other primary schools, including Nadia, Ms Anderson's daughter. They both passed. Nadia was able to take her place the following September at St John's Anglican Private School. Debbie, however, was unable to take up her place: her mother, still not working regularly and having difficulty making ends meet as it was, would never be able to afford the fees.

Grades 7 and 8

So when the time came, Debbie moved on to the government school, C.C. Sweeting Junior High, just along the road from Oakes Field Primary School. It was a great disappointment for Debbie not to be able to go to St John's, but she vowed to continue to do her best, keep her grades up and carry on taking every opportunity that came her way.

During the summer vacation, Ms Anderson bought the grey material for Nadia's St John's skirts. She bought enough material for three skirts. Ms Ferguson, on the other hand, was worried because she had no ready cash to buy the blue shirts and grey skirts that Debbie would need at C.C. Sweeting. She even wondered if Debbie would be able to start with the rest of the students in the first week of September.

Debbie, heavily involved in track practices and racing, was unaware of this problem. The thought of new school uniforms and where they would come from never entered her head. In this and most other instances, Ms Ferguson managed to hide their impoverished circumstances from her daughter; Debbie did not know of the struggle to keep her fed, presentable and tidy. She cannot remember ever being hungry: her mother always managed to send her to school with a breakfast in her stomach and a packed lunch to enjoy during the day.

When Ms Anderson arrived home with the new fabric, she called her daughter to show her. Nadia took one look at the material and immediately realised that it was not the correct shade of grey. 'Mommy, you've bought C.C. Sweeting grey fabric. St John's is a lighter grey.'

As soon as Nadia said it, Ms Anderson realised her mistake. She drove round to Debbie's house and held out the fabric. 'You're going to C.C.: take this material for your skirts.' Ms Ferguson was overcome with gratitude. 'How did you know, Ms Anderson? How did you know I couldn't afford the material for the skirts?'

'I didn't,' replied Ms Anderson, 'but it seems it's just as well I brought it round.'

'Thank you, thank you,' said the Fergusons together. Ms Ferguson often expresses her gratitude to Ms Anderson to this day for her act of great kindness.

Looking back on this incident, Debbie regards it as yet another of the fortunate events that have occurred in her life and kept her on what she sees as the predestined path to overcome so many of the adverse aspects of her childhood. This act of generosity meant, of course, that no matter what other items they might struggle to find, Debbie would at least have her school uniform ready for her first day at secondary school. This was approaching faster than either of them realised.

In the summer of 1988, Debbie left Oakes Field Primary School. In September, she walked through the gates of her new secondary school for the first time. Although she had previously expressed anxiety about going there, on her first morning she felt confident and happy. C.C. Sweeting School took the majority of its students from Oakes Field Primary and Debbie was among familiar faces.

A new homeroom teacher

On the first morning at her new school, Debbie sought out her friend from Oakes Field, Pamela Fox. They made their way to the office to find out which homeroom they had been assigned to and where they should go. They were to be in Ms Kay Albury's homeroom. C.C. Sweeting School is on two campuses, separated by Gregory Street. The older students in Grades 10–12 are taught in the buildings on the other side of the street, so would not feature in Debbie's early day-to-day life at the school.

From that first morning began another close, meaningful and lasting relationship between Debbie and her new teacher. Ms Albury was immediately impressed by her new student. She dedicated herself to succeeding and showed great perseverance at all times. 'Even at that time amongst those little seventh graders, she stood out,' remembers Ms Albury. 'You know, most youngsters in their first days at a new school are keen to impress and please their teachers, but Debbie was something else again. She stayed behind to talk to me. She came to the homeroom between classes to ask questions. She stayed in during break times so she could do the best work possible.'

As the weeks passed, Ms Albury came to see just how determined Debbie was to achieve all that she could. Through their conversations in the homeroom she learned of Debbie's background and humble origins. She discovered just how little the Fergusons had and how hard it was for them to survive. She learned how Debbie's mother placed so much emphasis on her daughter's education and gave up things for herself to make sure that Debbie had the books and writing materials she needed. 'That's something they brought up from Jamaica with them – the importance of school and learning.' Debbie's new uniform was always clean and pressed – Debbie looked after it herself even at this time – and she looked neat and presentable as a matter of course.

Ms Albury knew it was very rare to find such a highly focused attitude in one so young, especially at one of The Bahamas' government schools. 'Many of the young people in that system eventually achieve great things both academically and on the sports fields, but a large majority seem to lack the enthusiasm and the stamina to accomplish much more than the minimum in terms of qualifications,' she posits. 'It seems that many of the children in the junior high schools have little or no idea what they want out of school life and, if they have a clear goal in mind, lack the knowledge and the wherewithal to fulfil it. A large percentage too, want instant gratification – to get rich quick – without putting in the necessary hard work. Debbie was definitely an exception.' She began to respect her new seventh grader, not only for her desire to do well, but for her cheerful disposition and consistently positive attitude. Ms Albury has her own theory: 'At school everyone was equal. No matter what she had to go without at home – fancy clothes, snacks and extras in the food line, pocket money, music and television and other basic things – when she came to school, she was the equal of all the others, and thrived. She made sure she outdid them all academically. She never stopped until she made the 4.00 GPA, the maximum grade point average.'

It was obviously this approach, her constant striving for something better and never being satisfied with anything but the best she could produce, that made Debbie something special. When we add to that her polite and courteous manner, it is easy to understand why she made such a lasting impression on the faculty at C.C. Sweeting.

Ms Albury learned a lot about Debbie's early years in Jamaica from their conversations in their homeroom, and she too is convinced that the role models provided by her grandparents were crucial in establishing in Debbie's mind the desire to work hard and succeed. To work on, without complaint, even when the rewards are scant and times are hard, provided the backbone for Debbie's indomitable spirit and pushed her to excel.

'We spoke at least once every day,' says Ms Albury. 'And she would share all sorts of things with me. When she was happy, I would share her joy. When she was sad about anything, I would encourage her to look beyond today and search for the end of the rainbow.'

'It is very interesting, you know,' she adds, 'because Debbie became an inspiration for so many of the children in that class, especially her friend, Pamela. She pushed her and Pamela tried very hard to be like Debbie. She had such a humble way about her that the others never felt any jealousy or resentment towards her for her academic success. A lot of children who do well make sure that everyone knows they are the best, or they get a reputation for being cocky or arrogant, but not Debbie. Everybody liked her. She mixed with them all and she got on with them all.

'I have seen instances of children turning against the top student and real problems developing, with no one wanting to have anything to do with the bright ones. And often it's no fault of the clever or successful ones. But with Debbie, she inspired the others and many of them tried to be like her. There was never any resentment.'

Shortly after the Athens Olympics in 2004, Ms Albury bumped into her ex-student at Nassau International Airport. Ever enthusiastic, Debbie ran over and sat down with her for a chat and to catch up on each other's news. 'There I was,' states Ms Albury, 'sitting down with an Olympic bronze medallist who was treating me as if *I* were the champion. But that's how she's always been, so very friendly and humble and always pleased to see you. She has a way to make even the lowliest person feel special. Certainly her classmates in my homeroom felt privileged to have her there.'

Sports and academics

Academic success soon came to Debbie, but she was to make no less an impression on the sports field. All her classmates knew she was a star in the making and expected her to make waves, but the new sports teachers did not know her. Her reputation, gained that summer from her outstanding victory in the CAC Youth Championships, had preceded her. But the sports teachers did not know which student she was, nor did they realise what she was capable of.

In the first sports lesson of the new school year, the teachers arbitrarily split the students into groups, in preparation for the short fitness programme always taken by students at the beginning of the year. At C.C. there is a perimeter road that runs around the campus and Debbie's group was instructed to run around it as the first exercise.

Sports teacher Julie Wilson recalls that first session. 'I stood in the middle and watched them set off along the road. As Debbie stretched out in front of the others, I remember thinking, what incredible form! Even though she was only 12 at the time, I could tell that here was an athlete in the making. I set them another task on the road and she came in over half a lap ahead of all the others. She hardly seemed to be trying.'

Julie ran into the staff room and called out to one of her colleagues. This was Rupert Gardiner, another track and field specialist who has coached many young Bahamian athletes along with Pancho Rahming. 'Come out here quick,' she enthused, 'and watch this new seventh-grader.' Gardiner followed, watched Debbie easing along the road and told Julie that she must be the CAC athlete from Oakes Field about whom they had heard. They both continued to watch as Debbie ran, and both looked ahead to the inter-school track meets, to which she would undoubtedly contribute successfully.

From these first lessons it was soon obvious, however, that it would not only be track and field teams on which Debbie would make her mark. Julie Wilson also taught Debbie the finer points of netball. 'She was capable of playing everything. She was a strong and powerful hockey player, a real all-rounder. Some time after Debbie had left for St Andrew's, I remember taking a hockey team from C.C. up there to play a friendly match. Debbie was in their team. She had great ball sense, safe hands and her speed made her very difficult to guard with any success. This all-round ability can be a problem, of course, but she never let anything get in the way of her track commitments.'

It was, however, not her sporting prowess that really left a lasting impression on Julie Wilson. 'Above all,' she says, 'I remember her in those first few weeks because she was easily the politest and best-mannered student I have ever taught!' Julie Wilson has taught in The Bahamas for 26 years and, as a sports teacher, usually comes into contact with every girl in the school during the school year. Debbie impressed her because although she was unquestionably the most outstanding athlete in the seventh grade, she was quite happy for others to demonstrate particular skills and was always ready to help her peers learn how to throw or jump or hit a hockey ball. Wilson remembers, 'She could do it all, but she never pushed herself forward. She was happy for everyone to have their chance to shine.'

Wilson also remembers another day, soon after Debbie went to C.C. She was in the yard, with a different group of students, when the security guard came along, escorting a lady who wanted to see Mrs Wilson. Julie interrupted the class and turned to the lady, who introduced herself as Ms Ferguson, Debbie's mother. They exchanged pleasantries and then Ms Ferguson explained why she had come. 'I want you to know, Mrs Wilson, that while Debbie is here, she is to do as you teachers say. You are in charge of my child while she is here at school,' she told the sports teacher. 'If ever you have a problem with Debbie – if she doesn't do her work or she is rude – you are to send for me and I'll come and see to her.'

Wilson was very surprised by this: it is not common for parents to come to the school to check their children's progress, except on the regular parent–teacher conference evenings. It is even less common for parents to express such whole hearted support for the teachers. This was not an isolated incident: Ms Ferguson subsequently visited the school quite often, to see how Debbie was doing and to express again her confidence in the teachers. Clearly, this interest in her progress exhibited by her mother inspired Debbie to work hard and keep focused and went a long way to helping her to realise her potential.

Debbie achieved a 4.00 GPA during her Grade 7 year. It was the first time anyone had ever managed a perfect score at C.C. Sweeting. She also excelled at sports, of course. In her second CAC Youth Championships in the Cayman Islands, she won the overall title again. Her all-round talents were ideally suited to the CAC format and once again she made the most of the opportunity to display her abilities. Of course, the all-round ability was a benefit, but Julie Wilson explains one of the problems they had with Debbie at C.C. 'She was so good at so many events. In the inter-school track and field championships, we didn't know which ones to enter her for. She would probably have won them all, but we usually settled for the 100, 200 and 400 metres on the track, and the high jump and the long jump in the field.' Clearly, it was the kind of problem that many coaches and team selectors would love to have!

Meeting a legend

It was at this time, during the preparations for the CAC Championships, that Bahamian track and field legend Tommy Robinson first saw Debbie run.

Tommy Robinson represented The Bahamas in three Olympic Games and three Commonwealth Games, winning the gold medal in the 220-yard sprint in the 1958 Commonwealth Games in Cardiff, Wales. In the Commonwealth Games in Jamaica eight years later, he won the silver medal (but only after an astonishing 90-minute deliberation over the photo-finish). In 1981, he received the ultimate accolade from The Bahamas government when the stadium in the Queen Elizabeth Sports Centre was named the Thomas A. Robinson National Stadium in his honour. Tommy had competed against and beaten the best during his career. His background had certain similarities to Debbie's: he had lived, literally, 'Over-the-Hill'. His family home was on the south slope of Hawkins Hill, and from these humble beginnings, he had gone on to win a full track and field scholarship to the University of Michigan. By 1989 he was a respected and revered figure in track and field in The Bahamas.

Tommy Robinson spoke in measured tones, considering carefully every word, as if in direct disproportion to the speed with which he used to run. His knowledge of track and field and his ability to spot potential champions from his years of international exposure were unquestioned. Pancho Rahming first pointed Debbie out to Robinson while she was training for the CAC Games. It was immediately clear to him that he was watching a future star. 'It was her relaxation that really impressed me,' he explained. 'She never strained. Her head remained still and she seemed to be very much in control. For one so young – I think she was 13 at the time – this was a major advantage. Relaxation is key to good sprinting. It sometimes takes a long time to learn and it just seemed that she had developed this very early on. You see many athletes with talent who desperately seem to be trying to get their bodies to move faster. The more effort they put in, the less speed they produce. But with Debbie it just seemed to be effortless and very smooth.'

Watching Debbie that first time, Robinson was aware how much Pancho Rahming had achieved with her. He was quick to place the credit where it was due. 'Pancho coached her. He was responsible for all her training and all those good habits – her running form, her work ethic, her motivation – are really the results of his influence.'

When Debbie's session was over, Coach Rahming introduced her to Tommy. Like so many others, he was immediately taken with her friendliness and good manners. He describes it like this: 'Her personality shone through from the word go and she was so polite. "Yes, sir" and "No, sir" came as second nature to her. I took to her immediately and a long relationship was born that day. I was never involved with her training – Pancho took care of all that – but I like to think of myself as more of a mentor to her. Not so much about the track, but more about who she is and what she wants to do.

'Our upbringings have some similarities. I always impressed upon her that my beginnings were just as humble as hers and the area I lived in was just as poor as her Grant's Town home. I remember telling her that just because she lives in the ghetto doesn't mean the ghetto lives in her. She should be proud of herself and where she comes from. In fact, when she was about to go off to Georgia University, I spoke to her and told her that she was actually a little better off than me. When I went off to Michigan, I lived in a two-room house with an outhouse – at least she had a bathroom in the house!'

Debbie herself is quick to recognise the influence Tommy has had on her thinking and her ideas. 'Mr Robinson was another father figure in my life,' she acknowledges, 'and he was so very helpful and gave me assistance too often to remember. I am eternally grateful to him.'

Robinson, for his part, explained that he was only too pleased to offer assistance in any way he could, but still maintained that he felt more proud of the help he gave in less tangible, but more character-forming, ways. 'I was asked to sign a form when she went off to university as her legal guardian. That made me a sort of guarantor for her while she was there. In the absence of her real father, I was only too pleased to do it.

'But more important than that were the conversations I had with her about her future, and the importance of formulating a plan for the future when her track career was over. I tried to make her believe that with her ability on the track and her ability in the classroom, the world was hers for the taking. With Debbie and with many other budding track stars, I tried to instil in them the importance of being aware that track is a short career, so they need a back-up.

'I was fortunate enough to gain a scholarship to run at Michigan University, but it also gave me the opportunity to study for a career. Debbie had that advantage too. So when I speak to young, up-and-coming athletes, I encourage them for all I am worth to seek out possibilities like these and develop their talents in other fields. I told Debbie that at college, and while she competes around the world, opportunities will present themselves. She must make up her mind which way she wants to go. So I was an adviser really, someone to explain certain things to her.'

Tommy Robinson certainly practised what he preached: he became a successful businessman in Nassau, highly respected in the business community. Track and field remained his passion and he was actively involved in The Bahamas Amateur Athletic Association, but it was a hobby – one that he was dedicated to, but still a hobby. He explained from experience, 'My track career was a wonderful time – times, I should say – but what I learned at Michigan and the business ventures my studies led me to pursue are what have kept my family solvent, enabled me to buy a nice property and to send my kids to good schools. In fact, my daughter, Erica, was in the same grade as Debbie at St Andrew's. When I realised they would be classmates, I asked Erica to look out for Debbie and to try to help her settle into the school. I knew it would be something of a culture shock for her and wanted to do all I could to make the transition as easy as possible.'

Tommy Robinson's long and successful life came to an end in November 2012, when he passed away, aged 74. He was given a state-recognised funeral, at which a tribute was given by the Prime Minister.

After-school jobs

Back in Grade 8 at C.C. Sweeting, Debbie picked up from where she left off in Grade 7. She had the familiar figure of Ms Albury as her homeroom teacher and she remained very focused on her studies. Making her way home one evening after track practice, however, she passed one of Nassau's supermarkets, the Super Value food store on Nassau Street, and noticed a young girl, not much older than she was, carrying a bag of groceries out to a customer's car. Debbie stopped to watch and saw the customer give the girl some money for the service.

Packing boys and girls are a feature of Bahamian supermarkets. They work on a very unstructured basis, packing groceries at the check-out and then either carrying or wheeling the purchases out to the car park or, if the customer has no car, simply handing over the bags. In 1988, the customers probably gave the packing boys and girls 50 cents for their trouble.

Debbie thought it would help out at home if she could get some pocket money by packing bags for the couple of hours after track practice each evening before the store closed. She went into the store and asked the manager if she could work there. He told her to present herself the next evening.

As soon as she arrived home, she asked her mother if she could work as a packing girl. Her mother was not enthusiastic at first. 'You've got enough on your plate,' she told her daughter, 'without spending every evening packing groceries.' Debbie was determined to persuade her mother, but Ms Ferguson was not inclined to listen. 'You've made your four-point GPA and I wants you to keep it,' she reasoned. 'Have you stopped to think how tired you're going to be with your training and homework, and then this?'

'Please, Mommy,' Debbie must have repeated a hundred times, 'I just want to help.' Eventually, after her daughter had given assurances that her GPA would not drop and that she understood that if her schoolwork suffered, she would have to give up the job, Ms Ferguson reluctantly gave in and agreed.

So Debbie went to the supermarket the next evening after track practice and packed groceries for two hours until 9p.m. when the store closed, before going home and completing her homework and doing any other chores around the house. 'It was difficult to fit everything in,' she remembers. 'And I got to bed later than usual. But it felt good to bring home those few dollars each evening.'

This little job was to last for about six months until Ms Ferguson noticed that, despite all Debbie's efforts, there was indeed a drop in achievement in her schoolwork. She therefore told Debbie she must give it up. It was only a slight downturn, but enough to fall from the 4.00 which had given both mother and daughter so much pride.

Ms Ferguson paid one of her visits to the school and spoke to Ms Albury and Mrs Wilson, explaining the reason for Debbie's lower GPA. She also met the school's guidance counsellor, Mrs Joey Redhead, who was to play a key role in Debbie's scholarship to St Andrew's, recounted later in this chapter.

Again, Ms Ferguson explained the situation: 'That packing job in the evening made her too tired. I'm sorry she slipped from the 4.00.' Mrs Redhead, always positive and understanding, thanked Ms Ferguson for coming, told her not to worry and quietly stored away the information for future reference. Aware of the Fergusons' financial plight, she knew she had to do something to help if she could.

Unhappily, Debbie had to comply with her mother's instructions. She was upset that she had not been able to maintain her own standards at school. She was also upset that she was not going to be able to work anymore, because she liked the opportunity to meet people that it gave her. The money had come in handy, too. Nevertheless, it was not long before another chance meeting at the track and a fateful coincidence were to prove beneficial in both the short and the long term, and open many more doors along the way.

One evening after school, Debbie was practising the long jump and carefully measuring the distance in the sand. Pancho Rahming was supervising the activities and one of his older athletes, George Cleare, wandered over between repetitions to talk to him. Although he did not know Debbie, he asked her how far she had jumped and then playfully scattered some sand in her direction.

George remembers, 'She was wearing her C.C. uniform. We just played around for a few minutes in the sand, but we became friendly after that. We had the same coach so we came into contact quite regularly, even though I was concentrating on longer events like the 800 and 1500 metres.'

'We used to talk a lot at the track,' recalls Debbie, 'and sometimes George would walk along with me after practice. We got on very well. It was a sort of puppy love, I suppose, at first, and it lasted a long time, from 1990 until 2002! Of course, there were long stretches when we were apart – when I was away at college and the time when he was away too – but 12 years is a long time to be a couple. We were even engaged to be married at one point.'

At the time they met, George was still at school, but had a Saturday job with The Caribbean Bottling Company at the Coca-Cola plant. One evening, Debbie told him about the job she had had to give up at Super Value. He joked that she should try to get a job on Saturdays with him.

Debbie laughed with George at this suggestion, but inside she knew that a Saturday job would be the answer to many of her problems. There would be no rush to fit everything into the evenings and she would have longer to concentrate on her school work. There were rarely practices on Saturdays, so that would be ideal for a part-time job. Should she ask her mother about packing groceries at the store on Saturdays, she wondered? What would her mother say to such a suggestion?

In the meantime, Mrs Redhead, the guidance counsellor, had quickly put a plan into action. Her sister, Judy Munroe, happened to be Chief Executive Officer of The Caribbean Bottling Company, where George worked on Saturdays. A phone call to her sister explaining Debbie's situation, her personality and her future prospects was enough for Ms Munroe to find a Saturday job in the finance department for her sister's special student.

Judy Munroe is a member of ZONTA, an organisation that aims to advance the status of women. She spoke about employing Debbie on Saturdays to her financial controller, fellow ZONTA member and good friend, Earla Bethel. She asked Bethel if she could use her. 'There are always plenty of jobs to do in the finance department,' explains Bethel, 'filing, clerical things, answering the telephone, so I said to Judy, "Sure, bring her in."'

The necessary arrangements were made, Ms Ferguson made no objections and the next Saturday morning Judy Munroe escorted Debbie to the accounting department where she was introduced to Mrs Bethel. Debbie made an immediate impact with her willingness to learn and effervescent personality. 'She was so very polite,' enthuses Bethel, 'and extremely eager to learn and to please. In a very short time, I realised that she was a very special young girl.'

So, amazingly, Debbie found herself working at the same place as George on Saturday mornings (although he was in a different department). Having really done nothing herself to secure the job, Debbie was quite bewildered at the turn of events, but very grateful to everyone who had helped her to get the job. She set about doing her very best from the start, and worked energetically and competently in the accounting department for the next four years, until she left to go to the University of Georgia. She thoroughly enjoyed her time there: 'Actually, it wasn't only Saturday mornings; I would work there full-time during school vacations,' Debbie recalls, 'and I had a good time.'

Earla Bethel enjoyed having Debbie work for her too, and so began a relationship that has grown with the years. Mrs Bethel was another instrumental figure in Debbie's move to St Andrew's. Debbie receives inspirational emails from her even today and never misses an opportunity to call or visit her and her family. Bethel says, 'Through my involvement in ZONTA and friendship with Orinthia Nesbeth, I learned about the scholarship to St Andrew's. It was another of life's coincidences that my own two children, Danielle and Brad, were both at St Andrew's at that time, so this drew Debbie and me even closer. Once I realised just how difficult life was for her and her mom, I tried to do what I could in any way I could.'

Debbie readily acknowledges Earla Bethel's contribution to her development as a person and confirms that she did a tremendous amount for her all through high school. Debbie says, 'I admire Mrs Bethel so much. She is so professional. She is very successful, but she is very human. She invited me to their beautiful home and treated me just like her own daughter. I have taken other athletes there with me. I also have many conversations with her husband, who is a doctor, about studies at medical school. Danielle and Brad are like my own brother and sister. I feel part of their family. I am eternally grateful and I hope to be like her when I join the workforce in whatever capacity it may be.'

The admiration goes both ways because Bethel never ceases to sing Debbie's praises and hold her in high esteem for all that she has achieved, both on the track and in the classroom. She also reveres Debbie's character and willingness to give back to the community. After she won the gold medal in Sydney, Debbie told Bethel, 'Now it is time for me to do something for you. If ever you want me to help or do anything for your company, just let me know.'

Mrs Bethel is now the owner of a company which has the McDonald's franchise in Nassau. Debbie has kept her promise many times over. She has been invited to speak at staff training days, and each year, when McDonald's celebrates World Children's Day on 20 November, Debbie attends to play with the little ones, sign autographs and have her photo taken with the children. 'She never misses,' says Bethel. 'Just as it was at Coca-Cola, the McDonald's staff here love her and admire her. She often comes and talks to them and provides motivation and inspiration.

'In our training room we have a photo at the front of Debbie breaking the tape for the gold at the Sydney Olympics. Everyone can see it as they listen to the speakers. Our message to everyone is always, "If Debbie can do it, so can you."'

A growing interest in track and field

Back at school in January 1990, the C.C. Sweeting students were preparing for their inter-house sports, which serve as a trial for the later, more prestigious inter-school track and field championships. In the house competition Debbie won three events: the 100 metres in 12.29 seconds, the 200 metres in 25.38 seconds, and the long jump with a staggering 16 feet 9 inches (6.6 metres). This last record is a truly extraordinary statistic. Julie Wilson remarks, 'I'll bet there aren't many senior girls who can beat that, and remember, Debbie was only 13 at the time. With such a natural spring in her stride, who knows what she might have achieved if she had concentrated more on the long jump?'

Moving on to the inter-school championships, Debbie produced another stellar performance and made a huge contribution towards the C.C. Sweeting Cobras winning the title. 'We were very strong at that time,' Wilson says. 'Debbie was outstanding in her age group, but there were other girls who went on to represent The Bahamas at the CARIFTA Games: girls such as Altrece Taylor and Gill Aeneas, who were almost as good. When the three of them ran in the relay, we were an awesome team.' Indeed, C.C. Sweeting has a great reputation for track and field excellence, having won The Bahamas Government Secondary Schools Track and Field Championships many times since Debbie's contributions in 1989 and 1990. In fact, Debbie says unashamedly that she is a Cobra at heart and often returns to her old school to talk to the up-and-coming track athletes and wish them well.

After the Olympic success in 2000, as part of the victory celebrations, The Bahamas government sent the relay team – The Golden Girls, as they were called – to a number of schools. Each runner was allowed to choose two schools. Debbie chose the two secondary schools she had attended: C.C. Sweeting and St Andrew's. By that time, however, government reorganisation had led to C.C. becoming two separate schools, a junior high and a senior high. Since Debbie had attended the school when she was in grades 7 and 8, she visited the junior high on her celebratory tour.

Despite all the cheering, well-wishing and rejoicing, she managed to find the time to seek out Julie Wilson and tell her that she was sorry she had not been able to visit the senior high school. She promised Mrs Wilson that, if the opportunity ever arose again, she would visit the senior school. Four years later, after her bronze medal at the Athens Olympics, she was true to her word. She told the government officials that she did not care where else she went, but she had to go to C.C. Sweeting Senior High. So she celebrated with the students there before going once again to St Andrew's. In fact, such was the reception from the students and Debbie's involvement with them, taking photographs and signing autographs, that she kept the St Andrew's students waiting nearly an hour for their share in the jubilation!

CHAPTER 3
ST ANDREW'S SCHOOL: A SCHOLARSHIP

Scholarship opportunity

Until 1948, the premier private institution in The Bahamas was Queen's College. When the college decided to accept black students in 1949, a group of rich, white merchants reacted by setting up another school. This became St Andrew's, and for many years it had an unwritten racist policy not to allow black students. Unsurprisingly, it was often been referred to as a 'snobby, white school'. Its fees were the highest in The Bahamas, which served to maintain its policy. As more black families were financially able to move into the upper middle class, however, black students began to win places and attend the school. At the time that the Bahamas General Certificate of Secondary Education, the BGCSE, replaced the Cambridge University Overseas O levels, the school replaced Queen's College as the top academic school in the Bahamas in terms of exam results and college places attained. Over time, it gained recognition as the best private school in The Bahamas.

In 1980, the Board of Directors was sufficiently enlightened to set up a programme to offer academic scholarships to a small number of students from government schools. Initially the scholarships were for the final two years of schooling, but with the introduction in 1993 of the BGCSE, which meant compulsory twelfth-grade education, the scholarships were granted for the final three years.

Three events were instrumental in Debbie's move to St Andrew's. The first was the achievement of Mrs Orinthia Nesbeth, the owner of General Brokers Insurance Agency in Nassau, and a person with strong philanthropic views. She had been working to arrange financing for a full scholarship for a deserving government school student to attend a private school in Nassau. The money was to come from a Trinidadian company with which she had been doing business for some years, and was to fund complete secondary schooling, rather than the final three years. The particular school had not been decided, but there would be enough funding for any of Nassau's private schools. Mrs Nesbeth wanted the scholarship to go to a student who would make the most of the opportunity and, just as importantly, would uphold certain positive characteristics such as humility, conscientiousness, politeness and adaptability.

The second event was when Mrs Nesbeth consulted her good friend and fellow ZONTA club member, Joey Redhead, the guidance counsellor at C.C. Sweeting. When Mrs Nesbeth told her she had funds for a scholarship and asked if there were any suitable students at C.C. Sweeting, Mrs Redhead happened to mention a seventh-grade student who was achieving great things both in and out of the classroom – maintaining a 4.0 grade point average (the first student in the history of the school to achieve this) and representing The Bahamas on the track.

The third, and most important, event was Mrs Redhead's arrangement for Mrs Nesbeth to meet Debbie in a formal interview. She naturally wanted to assess this candidate for the scholarship and to determine if she was worthy. The recommendation from C.C. Sweeting included information about Debbie's academic ability. Mrs Nesbeth also knew that the girl was a track star in the making, but she wanted to see for herself what kind of person Debbie was.

The interview took place in Mrs Nesbeth's office and after only a few minutes of conversation, she knew her search was over. There was no doubt that this was the girl for the scholarship. So impressed was she by Debbie's positive yet humble attitude, her polite and mannerly approach, and her friendly and positive personality that she felt certain that not only would Debbie benefit from the opportunity, but that any school she went to would be enriched by her attendance.

There just remained the choice of private school. For Mrs Nesbeth there was really no contest, as she had long been impressed by the academic record of St Andrew's, the only completely independent school in The Bahamas. In addition, her husband Lloyd's regular squash partner, Roger Kelty, was the deputy principal and head of the secondary school at St Andrew's. Finally, acquaintance, through ZONTA, with Earla Bethel, who had two children at the school, confirmed her opinion and her conviction that it provided the best education available.

We must not forget that it was an academic scholarship that was being awarded, so as far as Mrs Nesbeth was concerned, athletics came a very definite second to the academic opportunities. In fact, St Andrew's did not have an impressive record for sport at that time, and there were other schools with far more impressive sporting credentials. This did not deter Mrs Nesbeth from her decision. Her view was that, 'At this time Debbie liked to run, but I felt nevertheless that, for the type of girl Debbie was, St Andrew's was the best school for her.' The next thing was to arrange an interview at the school. After one of their regular squash games, Lloyd Nesbeth mentioned to Roger Kelty, who was in charge of admissions at St Andrew's, that his wife had a scholarship available to pay for a student of whom she thought very highly. The arrangements were made for Debbie to come to the school to be interviewed. 'So we interviewed her,' says Roger, 'and she was just outstanding. We knew nothing about her athletic ability, she was just a really nice personality: so mannerly and friendly and willing to talk and explain herself fully. And we accepted her without any questions. It was really as simple as that.'

It may have seemed that simple to Roger Kelty, but he had not bargained for Ms Ferguson's reaction to the prospect of her daughter moving to the island's most expensive private school. She was understandably both excited and worried. She was aware of the opportunities that the school would provide for her daughter, but she was also aware of the social pressures of being surrounded by children from far more privileged backgrounds. Debbie was just 12 at the time St Andrew's offered her a place. Ms Ferguson feared that Debbie was too young. She felt that a move now, when things were going so well academically at C.C. Sweeting, might be detrimental to Debbie's progress.

She also believed that the culture shock on a 12-year-old who lived in what was, and still is, labelled 'the ghetto' could possibly be quite traumatic. She talked it over with Mrs Nesbeth. When she was told that both the scholarship and the place at St Andrew's could be held over, she decided that Debbie should stay at C.C. Sweeting until the summer of 1990, the end of her eighth grade, when she would be a little older and better able to handle the social pressures.

Meanwhile, the teachers at C.C. Sweeting viewed Debbie's scholarship and future at St Andrew's with mixed feelings. They agreed unanimously that the school would provide excellent opportunities for her. On the other hand, they were a little upset to be losing their outstanding academic student.

We should note here that the little hiccup that occurred at the beginning of Grade 8 as far as the GPA was concerned was resolved after Debbie gave up the evening job and started working on Saturdays instead. Her determination to put it back where she felt it belonged caused her GPA to bounce back to the 4.00 of Grade 7. She left C.C. with a more than outstanding academic record.

As far as the athletics was concerned, her coaches at C.C. knew she was destined for great things. They felt comfortable that her work with Pancho Rahming would keep her on course for a superlative career on the track. They were disappointed that Debbie would no longer be a member of the Cobras teams, but were assured that she would not be competing against them in future championships because St Andrew's took part in the Independent Schools Championships, and did not compete against the government schools. As for the national championships, St Andrew's hardly ever sent competitors there, so C.C. was probably still going to be strong enough to claim its usual double victory.

An important event for Debbie in the summer of 1990 was selection for her first CARIFTA Games. Although only 13, she made the qualifying time and was elated to be part of the team. She was doubly pleased because it meant going back to Jamaica, the land where she had spent her early childhood. She did not compete in any individual events, but did participate in the 4×100-metre relay. Debbie's memories of this event are very vague: she just remembers that she went back to Jamaica for the first time since moving to Nassau nearly four years earlier. As a 13-year-old competing in the under-17 age group, she was, to a large extent, out of her depth, and could not have competed on an individual basis. The exposure in the relay was nevertheless beneficial and an experience she would not have missed.

Debbie's time at C.C. came rapidly to an end. Sooner than she anticipated, it was time to say farewell to teachers and friends. The school year was ending and a new era of her life was about to begin. The summer vacation arrived and Debbie closed the book on C.C. Sweeting, with a number of track records to her name and a 4.00 GPA to immortalise her for future students at the school.

Debbie hugged Ms Albury and said goodbye, promising to return to tell her what St Andrew's was like at the first opportunity. She walked out of the gate she had entered two years previously, little realising what a huge step she was about to take. After a summer of working at Coca-Cola, she would discover just how different the world she was moving into would be.

The school bus

St Andrew's is located at the very eastern end of the island of New Providence and about eight miles from the centre of Nassau. Debbie's home in Grant's Town was about the same distance from the school. The distance from her home to C.C. Sweeting School was about a mile and Debbie walked, or ran, there happily every day. Walking to St Andrew's would be out of the question. Consequently, getting to school in the mornings was not going to be easy. There was public transport, of course, the famous Nassau jitney bus service, but that would involve catching at least two buses in each direction and a cost of two dollars a day, or ten dollars a week. The Fergusons could not spare that sort of money.

The other problem was the time it would take. To reach St Andrew's by 8.30 in the morning, catching two buses, Debbie would have to leave home by 7.30. That would cut into her early morning training sessions. Travelling from the east to the stadium for after-school training sessions would also be difficult and time-consuming, and this was an additional cause for concern. Would she be able to get there in time for the evening workouts? How much would the travel time cut into her homework time?

For a while, Debbie did not know how she would solve these conundrums, but, in the end, as with so many things, the solution was very simple. As soon as Mrs Nesbeth heard of Debbie's concerns, she arranged for her to take one of the school charter buses that served the various private schools, and willingly paid the monthly charge. 'I could not have our first scholarship student worrying about how she was going to get to and from St Andrew's,' she says. 'It seemed only natural to use the school bus, and it made life so much easier for Debbie.'

Debbie remembers certain aspects of her first day at St Andrew's quite vividly. Dressing in her new navy blue skirt in the tiny, wooden Wilson Street house, and slipping on her first ever pair of Clarks school shoes. She was ready an hour before the bus was due to collect her. Those Clarks shoes were her pride and joy – something she had dreamed of owning, but had never been able to afford. She had Mrs Bethel to thank for those, and for her brand new backpack, and the pristine uniform that she wore with a mixture of pride and apprehension on that first day.

Having no idea what to expect, Debbie felt an avalanche of emotions as she waited for Miller's Bus Service jitney to call for her. Lack of transport meant that she had been unable to go back to the school to familiarise herself with the physical structure, and, knowing no one else at the school, she was unable to formulate any ideas about her new schoolmates. What would the students be like? Would she fit in with them? What about the teachers? Would they like her? Would she like them? Would she be the only black student in her class?

These are usual questions on a student's first day at a new school, but Debbie had other things to contend with that she had not anticipated. She knew that she lived in a poor neighbourhood, but the bus journey on that first day threw into clear perspective the gulf that existed between her environment and that of most of the other children at St Andrew's.

When Debbie took her place in Grade 9 in 1990, the ratio of black to white students in the upper grades was approximately 1:1. Only in the St Andrew's Primary School section was it possible to clearly detect the old white majority. At this time, the atmosphere of the school was changing, and although most of the students still came from wealthy backgrounds, there were also a number of students whose parents were teachers or blue-collar workers making huge sacrifices because they wanted the best education possible for their children. Somewhat unfairly, however, the 'snobby, white' image remained. No matter how many black students took up places at the school, and no matter how many local and national activities St Andrew's students took part in with students from other government or private schools, the slurs of snobbery, racism and elitism remained among a large proportion of the Bahamian public.

In Debbie's Grade 9 homeroom were the sons and daughters of doctors, lawyers, bank managers and entrepreneurs, along with psychiatrists, permanent secretaries in The Bahamas government and successful property developers.

When the bus stopped to pick up Debbie on that first morning, it was only half full and she took an empty seat at the front. As it pulled away, she heard one or two comments about the new girl and the area she lived in, but she did not respond – it was her first day, after all. The bus then made its rounds, picking up other students, and as they emerged from what seemed to Debbie to be ever grander and more expansive homes, standing in spacious, beautifully manicured grounds, she became more and more impressed and gazed in awe at the houses. 'Wow!' she thought, 'if only that home could be mine. This is the house I dream of ... and these are my new school mates!'

In fact, these new school mates on the bus provided the first situations of conflict that she would face in her new environment. As the days passed, the comments about where she lived became more pointed, until she was stung to retaliate. Debbie says, 'Going to school at C.C., you have to be tough to survive and I felt tomboyish and rough and ready compared to these "refined" ladies and gentlemen on the bus. But when they started talking about my area and asking about this girl from the ghetto, I had to put them straight. I told them that their fine houses did not give them the right to talk about me as they did. They did not know me or anything about me, so I just told them not to say anything about me. I didn't do it any bullying way, but firmly enough so they knew I meant it. Funnily enough, it seemed to do the trick, because very quickly, in just a week or so, the remarks stopped and all of us on the bus became really close and friendly. They came to know me as a person and I think they respected me for what I had said.'

This served as a real learning experience for the young Debbie, who, ever since then, has believed in speaking her mind and saying things as she feels them. In this way, the air is always clear and everyone knows exactly where they stand. However, this went very much against what her mother had told her a few weeks earlier. Ms Ferguson was anxious for Debbie to fit in at St Andrew's and not to appear out of place. She had told Debbie to maintain a low profile: 'Don't draw attention to yourself, girl,' she told her daughter. 'When you gets there, if you sees them other students jumping up and down on one and a half legs, then you jump up and down on one and a half legs!'

Debbie had agreed with her mother that this was the way to go, but her pride and the words Tommy Robinson had spoken to her when he first met her had quickly moved her to stick to her principles, even if it meant answering back to other students. 'That taught me never to be ashamed or afraid to stick up for myself,' she says. 'When people realise you're being honest and true to your own beliefs, they respect you more.'

A challenging new world

The bus dropped Debbie and her companions on the grass by the netball courts: Debbie had arrived for her first day. There were, of course, many other 'rookies' on that September morning, boys and girls, and Debbie joined the throng walking to the assembly hall, where they would find out their homerooms and who were to be their classmates for the year. Debbie felt small and anonymous sitting in the hall waiting to hear her name called. She knew no one and no one knew her. Some of the faculty members knew there was a new girl in Grade 9 who was a CARIFTA athlete, but no one knew what she looked like and no one paid her any more attention than any of the other new students. While it was all new to Debbie, she did not feel self-conscious or strange in any way. 'We were all a bunch of kids starting a new school year,' is how she reflects on the moment.

She left the hall with her new classmates and made her way to her homeroom and immediately felt at home. The returning students were very friendly, and Debbie's own ability to communicate and respond to positive vibrations allowed her to fit in from the moment they reached the classroom. She managed to replace any feelings of uneasiness with a feeling of confidence, inspired by what she saw as genuine friendship from her classmates. They were impressed by her too, because she was not shy and talked openly and happily with everyone. Her classmates had no idea she was an international athlete, and her own modesty prevented her from mentioning it, but her athletic talent naturally revealed itself in the first sports lesson. Students in her class recall being astounded by the new girl's speed on the track, her hitting power in games of softball, and her tenacity on the hockey field. She stood out no matter what she did.

After the first sports lesson, the teacher organised a quick race back to the changing rooms, boys against girls, and Debbie shocked everyone by beating the fastest of the boys in what was a race of about 200 metres! It was Debbie's powerful running in this 'race' that led the boys to nickname her 'Horse', a name that stuck throughout high school. Some years later, when she was seen on television preparing to run in the Sydney Olympics, many of her classmates were amused to see a tattoo of a stallion on her thigh. Debbie says it is not because of the nickname *per se*, but she concedes that subconsciously she might have been reminiscing on her schooldays when she had it done.

As had been the case in her previous two schools, Debbie's sporting talent was the passport to acceptance, with the official stamp provided by her friendliness and willingness to socialise with everyone, both boys and girls, easing her through the immigration department of approval among her new peers.

There was just one sport at which she could not shine. Arriving at St Andrew's as a non-swimmer, Debbie was in a very small minority. The school had a 25-metre pool and a very good reputation as a swimming school, but Debbie was destined to be confined to splashing around in the shallows, and guarding the goal in the shallow end in water polo. Try as she might, even four years of swimming lessons did not make her anything but a novice swimmer. She did persevere in her usual determined fashion, though, and she did manage to conquer her fear of the water before she graduated.

Academically, and in all the different groupings for particular subjects, Debbie settled in well and was quickly recognised as one of the group. There was, however, one aspect at St Andrew's with which she had to come to terms. At C.C. Sweeting she had regularly gained As and, as we have seen, achieved the perfect 4.00 GPA before she left. At St Andrew's, academic competition was much greater and no one had ever achieved the perfect GPA. Debbie had to come to terms with not making As so regularly.

'That was a big adjustment,' she says somewhat ruefully. 'Actually, there were plenty of big adjustments. One was getting used to being in the middle of the class; at C.C., I had always been at the top. Another was accepting grades like B and B–, especially in subjects like English and maths. Another was feeling humbled by some of the other really smart kids in my class. I remember thinking, "I can't believe it. These kids are so smart." This is where I felt St Andrew's was a different world. There were lots of students in the grade who were very high achievers. I had to fight to get myself amongst them.'

Humbled or not, Debbie soon began to make her mark academically. Her work ethic and determination to improve impressed her teachers and gained the respect of her peers. Her habit of staying after the bell to ask for clarification on parts of the lesson showed all her teachers just how conscientious she was.

Her peers, on the other hand, remember her sprinting from class to class, carrying her backpack full of books, almost as if each lesson change was an opportunity for some more training! Some teachers remember that she often supplemented the weight of the books in her backpack with rocks, so that running with it to lessons and walking with it around the campus strengthened her leg muscles.

Others remember her voracious appetite. 'Debbie was always eating,' some will tell you. 'For one so small, she ate a lot. In fact, she ate a phenomenal amount – before school, during class changeovers and during lunch breaks. She ate a lot, and it wasn't particularly healthy food. She loved the peas 'n' rice, the hot patties and the fried chicken.'

This endearing picture has remained in the minds of those who were at school with her. Now they realise that rising before six in the morning and training for an hour, going to the track in the afternoons and training for two more hours, then going home to study and complete homework assignments necessitated a high fuel intake. Debbie made sure she ate enough to see her through.

It was Earla Bethel, once again, who contributed much to her daily food supply: she always sent three sets of food each day, one for each of her own children and the third for Debbie!

Teething problems

In 1990, when Debbie was settling in at St Andrew's, the Bahamas Association of Independent Secondary Schools (BAISS) was beginning to develop its own competitive sports programme. At the time, competition was limited to softball, soccer, swimming, and track and field. By 2005, the programme had grown to six major competitions: softball, soccer, volleyball, basketball, swimming, and track and field.

Debbie represented St Andrew's in softball and track. At the BAISS track meets, she contributed a large percentage of the St Andrew's points. She was never beaten in the 100 or the 200 metres, and also won the 400 metres on three occasions. One year, she had been entered for five events, and had already won the 100 metres, 200 metres, 400 metres and long jump when the girl who had been entered for the high jump twisted her ankle warming up. Debbie recalls Jane Butcher, the sports teacher, anxiously looked around for a replacement, someone who could score a couple of points for the school simply by taking part. She looked in Debbie's direction, and from the look on Debbie's face, realised that she need look no further. 'Just do it so we score something,' Debbie remembers Miss Butcher saying encouragingly.

Miss Butcher, however, had not taken into account either Debbie's competitive nature or her innate athletic ability. Debbie skipped over to the high-jump area, rehearsing in her mind what she had seen the high-jump specialists doing at the track in the evenings, took a couple of practice jumps, and proceeded to win the event without breaking sweat! So much for a couple of points for taking part! It was the same every year. She was always willing selflessly to step into the breach if it meant helping the St Andrew's team. By the time the BAISS Championships came around in March 1994, Debbie's final year, her talent and reputation preceded her. She was expected to win everything.

By this time, she had become an integral part of the St Andrew's class, loved and respected not only by her peers and her teachers, but also by the parents of the students in her class. Over time, they had watched her performances for St Andrew's, seen her run for The Bahamas in the 1992 CARIFTA Games held in Nassau, and met her at a number of school functions and birthday parties organised by her friends. Some of them had driven her and a group of friends to the movies, the bowling alley or out for pizza. These parents embraced her as one of their own, felt a part of her successes and watched her developing talent avidly.

At the track there were whisperings of a scholarship to a US university. On one of the three days of competition, a large group of parents from a number of the different schools were in the VIP area discussing the various student athletes. Debbie Ferguson was mentioned. A parent from another school expressed the view that Debbie had changed, becoming snobby and aloof, and forgetting where she came from since she had moved to that 'white school'. A small group of St Andrew's parents were incensed by the inaccuracy of the comment. Ever ready to stick up for their star student, they told the parent in strong language that this was complete nonsense and that she should check her facts before making such inflammatory remarks.

Debbie's popularity and acceptance by the entire St Andrew's community were, however, a long way off when she was adjusting to life at St Andrew's back in 1990. At the end of her first week, excited and encouraged by the reception she had received from students and faculty alike, she returned to C.C. Sweeting to see her old teachers and give them her initial impressions. Her excitement and happiness in reporting the good things about her first week were matched by the teachers' pleasure in hearing the good news: it reinforced their feelings that her move to the far east of the island would ultimately prove to be the right one.

Nevertheless, in those days, there was always some adjustment to be made or matter that she would have to address. The first PTA meeting of the year provided one more example. Coming very quickly after the new school year started, the evening meeting provided an opportunity for parents of new students to find out about the non-academic aspects of life at St Andrew's and to feel part of their children's new environment. Debbie took home the letter of invitation. She was obviously keen to be represented at the meeting, but Ms Ferguson refused to entertain the idea. She was anxious and could not imagine herself among a group of parents from a school like St Andrew's.

Feeling upset and let down, Debbie did not know what to do. Ever resourceful, however, she went back to see Mrs Wilson at C.C. Sweeting to see if she could give any words of advice or suggest a solution. She arrived at Mrs Wilson's office tearful and flustered, but managed to explain to her old sports teacher that she really wanted someone to go to the PTA on her behalf: it was the first meeting. Julie Wilson thought she might have a solution and went home with Debbie to speak to Ms Ferguson. 'Ms Ferguson,' she asked, 'will you go to the PTA meeting if I go with you? Debbie really wants you to be there, so will you come with me?'

At first, Ms Ferguson seemed to agree, but eventually her anxieties about the type of people she would see there and her fears about what she might face proved too much. She could not pluck up enough courage and would not go. So Julie Wilson went on her behalf, and at the end of the evening she introduced herself to Debbie's homeroom teacher, Judy Reiach, and explained why she was there. She told Mrs Reiach that plenty of persuasion and coaxing would be necessary to persuade Debbie's mother to attend these meetings. Judy Reiach said that she would do what she could to encourage Ms Ferguson to attend. Having her mother attend the PTA was obviously another way that Debbie felt she would be accepted by the school.

By the time of the next meeting, two important things had happened. Debbie had made her first really close friend, Tracee Rolle, eldest daughter of a man who would become a member of parliament in the general election in 1992. Mrs Reiach had also spoken to Ms Ferguson about attending the next PTA evening. Debbie had already met Tracee's parents and her mother had dropped Debbie home a couple of times. She had therefore met Ms Ferguson, so there would be a couple of familiar faces to make her feel more at home in the auditorium.

Nevertheless, Ms Ferguson was still unwilling to go alone, and only agreed to attend if Julie Wilson accompanied her. Julie willingly complied, and Ms Ferguson saw Tracee Rolle's mother and was introduced to a few more of Debbie's classmates. The trepidation and anxiety dissolved. She never again felt awkward or nervous about attending school functions. Indeed, as Debbie's friendship with Tracee grew and they become really close, so did the relationship between their mothers. Mrs Rolle became another willing and ready supporter of the family and regularly helped them through the many tough financial times. These times were made more difficult by Ms Ferguson's declining health and her resultant inability to work. She continued to sell frozen drinks and candies, and she still had babies to take care of from time to time, but some weeks it seemed to Debbie that their only money came from her 50 dollars for working at the Coca-Cola factory on a Saturday.

Debbie did not let anything distract her from her goals, however, and her first year at the new school began to take positive shape. As time went on, she began to feel even more at home. The number of her friends increased among the student body, as did the respect she gained from members of the faculty who taught her.

Roger Kelty remarks, 'It was wonderful to watch the way the students took to her right away. She was always so positive and friendly with everyone. I do remember one morning though, when she appeared at my office door in floods of tears. I asked her to come in and tell me what was wrong. She explained that money was very short because her mother was not working. She thought

74

they were going to be evicted from their house because they were in arrears with the rent. I tried to comfort her and told her I would do all I could to help.

'She left feeling much better, but, to be honest, I didn't know how I was going to do anything to assist. Then I had a brainwave and called a Rotary Club friend, Durward Knowles. Of course, he's Sir Durward now. I explained the situation to him and he wrote a cheque there and then to cover the arrears and the next month's rent. That sort of thing was absolutely typical of the man – I can't begin to tell you how many people Durward has helped – and he never wants anyone else to know about it.'

It is worth mentioning here that Sir Durward was The Bahamas' first Olympic gold medallist, having won a sailing gold in the Star class at the Tokyo Olympics in 1964. Debbie had no idea how the rent was paid.

While there were continual financial problems, Debbie's running maintained its steady and irresistible progress. Over the Easter weekend in 1991, the annual CARIFTA Games were held in Trinidad and, once again, Debbie qualified by times for the team. She was still young though, even for the under-17 age group, and still entered the competition with a certain amount of trepidation. Once in Port of Spain, all nervousness evaporated. 'I let my running do the talking,' Debbie explains. She served notice of her potential to the rest of the Caribbean by making it to the finals of both the 100 and the 200 metres.

'I made the finals of both the 100 and the 200, and I actually won the 100 metres. I still regard that as one of my greatest achievements. I was still young and I won the gold. In the 200 final, I came third. I guess I wasn't quite strong enough for the longer race. But I really felt I had arrived by getting these medals, and I could see I was improving all the time.'

75

Despite the positive development of her running, there were still difficulties at home. Ms Ferguson remained in ill health and was unable to work for the rest of the school year, but Debbie progressed smoothly and there were no further problems with the rent.

At school, she coped very well in some subjects – chemistry, health science and history – but really had to work in English and maths. As already mentioned, there were always other adjustments that she had to make. Even in the early 1990s, when it was largely a matter of landlines, using the phone was a hobby for young people. Like any others, St Andrew's students used it as an extension of their school days, to talk about the day, compare notes, test each other for class quizzes that were coming up, and just to chat. Before Christmas in her first term, Debbie was in a group working on a physics project. When the class ended, one of the students told Debbie she would call her that evening to finish the project. This was normal. At first, Debbie didn't quite know how to respond, but then blurted out, 'But Charelle, we don't have a phone.' Charelle was dumbfounded. 'You don't have a phone?'

'Well, *we* don't, but there's a lady at the back of our yard who has one and we sometimes use that,' replied Debbie. Charelle, now a doctor at Nassau's Princess Margaret Hospital, realised that the situation was embarrassing for Debbie, so she did not pursue that line of conversation. It served to point out to her, however, the gulf between her way of life and Debbie's, and it brought home to her the things that she took for granted and never even thought about. Needless to say, they completed the project – but not over the phone.

Debbie also had to adjust to many of the topics of conversation enjoyed by her peers. She remembers that the movie *The Color Purple* had made a big impression. Her classmates were talking about it one day, not because they had been to the movies, but because they had watched it on satellite TV. Debbie reflects, 'They all had satellites and could choose from hundreds of channels. We had a television, but half the time the reception was very bad. When we could watch it, we just had ZNS, the Bahamian channel, and nothing else. I thought, oh my God, they have all these things... but the funny thing is that we all got along. It was fine. They never made me feel that I didn't belong.'

At times, she found the long days – rising at five in the morning and sometimes not getting to bed until past midnight – too tiring. But she never missed a day of school and always managed to submit assignments on time. She was beginning to make a big impression on the St Andrew's community – teachers and students alike – and by the end of the year, with a grade point average of 3.40, she made the honour roll. 'I was very pleased with that,' she says. 'Not overjoyed, because I wanted to do better, but for the first year among all those smart kids, I was pleased.' She had also played a full part in extracurricular sport, somehow finding the time after school to stay behind and play for school and house teams. She was a member of the school softball team and represented her house, Arawak, in all the sports, including keeping goal in the water polo competition.

Predictably, she won all her events at the inter-house track and field competition, but the victory that gave her the most pleasure during her first year was in the School Run, an event featuring every student in the secondary section of the school. It was a race over a course of about a mile that began inside the school campus, went out through some nearby streets and then finished back inside the school grounds. For Debbie, it was her first competitive race over such a long course, but she won with consummate ease and hardly seemed out of breath at the end. She hastened to tell her housemaster afterwards, however, that she was not going to make a habit of racing over such a distance, and hoped that he would not select her for distance races in the inter-house track and field competition.

The field trip: Andros 1991

Coming back for Grade 10 in September 1991, Debbie already felt like an old hand, comfortable on the bus, happy and well respected by her peers. She had made her option choices for courses that she would study for the public exams, and she had chosen the subjects best suited for the career of paediatrician that she was determined to follow after St Andrew's.

This was also the year of what was to become the infamous environmental studies field trip to Andros, one of the Family Islands of The Bahamas. The school had been going to the centre at Forfar for a number of years. Many students had enjoyed the rustic way of life and the unspoiled environment of a Bahamian out-island. Debbie looked forward to the trip keenly, but was unsure how she was going to pay for it. There was no spare money at home for such a luxury, but once again help came from the ZONTA ladies, in the form of sponsorship for the trip.

'It was amazing. I don't remember ever actually telling Mrs Nesbeth or Mrs Bethel about these things, but they always seemed to know. Somehow they knew and always paid every bill,' says Debbie, somewhat disbelievingly.

The students set off for Andros, where they studied beaches, mangroves, sea life and plant life during the day, and enjoyed social activities in the evenings. After one evening activity, Debbie and a group of her friends went for a walk along the beach. It was a moonless night and the sky was very dark, the sort of dark you only find in places where there is no spillage of electric light. The girls carried torches, but held on to each other tightly to avoid tripping over. They were joking about ghosts and phantoms when, suddenly, the beam of one of the lights reflected off a shiny metallic surface. Another beam revealed the sinister figure of a man standing ominously on the sand. Startled at being discovered, the man hastily hid the metallic object into his trouser pocket and swore at the girls. They were more than a little scared.

Was it a gun? A knife? They did not recognise the man, but did not think he was one of the people who worked at the centre. They were afraid they were going to be attacked, and screamed. The man shouted and swore at them again. Seeing the fear on the faces of her friends, Debbie immediately began to berate the man, who was a stranger and should not have been loitering around the camp. She felt protective of her classmates in this situation and was not going to let anyone bully the other girls.

'I grew up in the ghetto,' she explains, 'and a lot of these St Andrew's girls were very sheltered. I decided I would look out for them. I stood up against this intruder. We thought he might have had a weapon, so I had to do something to show that he could not frighten us like this.'

The other girls were amazed by the venom in Debbie's attack and the angry tone in which she shouted at him. It was the only occasion in her four years at St Andrew's that the famous temper her mother speaks of revealed itself. The other girls were stunned into silence. Certainly, the man was abashed enough to run off, never to be seen again, but Debbie's anger was not quenched so quickly. She was enraged. The tears flowed profusely. Three of the girls had to hold her back as she was about to follow the man, and then reinforcements were called to lead Debbie back to the cabin. So incensed was Debbie that this man had disrupted their evening and threatened their safety, that two girls had to literally sit on her to prevent her from going back to the beach. Ultimately, she calmed down enough for the girls to take her to the staff cabin, where the teachers, who had also been very upset by the incident, talked to her and began to calm her down. As a result of this sympathetic counselling, the tears stopped and Debbie eventually regained her equilibrium. When she returned to the students' cabin, everyone was worried about how she felt. There were hugs all round. While the other girls had been shocked at the vehemence she had shown, her standing up to the man and defence of her friends gained her more respect and cemented the friendships even more securely.

Two years a senior

Over the Easter weekend, in April 1992, the annual CARIFTA Games were held in Nassau. Debbie was selected for The Bahamas team, and for many of her St Andrew's friends and teachers this provided the first opportunity to watch her compete at international level. She did not let anyone down. In a display of determined, top-class sprinting, she won the Under-17 Division 100 metres in 11.79 seconds, came second in the 200 metres (on a very windy day) in 23.79 seconds and also finished second in the 400 metres, in 54.68 seconds.

Debbie recalls her achievements: 'I was especially pleased with the 400 metres result, as it represented a new departure for me and one that Coach Rahming had wanted to implement for some time. I ran very well in the 100 metres, but in the 200 I felt the wind coming off the bend and couldn't maintain my stride as I wanted to. I was leading at that time, but that little blip in my form let another runner past me.'

Pancho Rahming was enthusiastic about her performance, feeling that it justified his belief that the longer race could actually be Debbie's best distance. They had developed a training schedule for it and Debbie had responded well. She was not slow, however, in telling her coach that she did not want to continue to train for the 400.

'It really hurts,' she says. 'It's only twice the 200 metres, but it feels like three or four times as far, especially in the last 50 metres. To be honest, the 100 and the 200 are painful enough at times and I really didn't want that sort of hurt on a regular basis. I don't mind running in the 4×400 relay from time to time, but to put myself through the extra training consistently was something I told Mr Rahming I didn't want to have to contend with.'

So the experiment was stopped. It's worth mentioning here, however, that Debbie's long-time friend and eventual Georgia University colleague, Tonique Williams, who won the 400 metres Olympic gold in Athens, was running the 400 metres in that same CARIFTA Games and Debbie beat her quite comfortably. Who knows what she may have achieved at the longer distance if she had not preferred the shorter sprints?

After the Easter break and the exertions of the CARIFTA Games, it was back to school. Two things dominated the students' thinking: the tenth-grade examinations and the selection of prefects. The St Andrew's tradition at the time was to elect the following year's prefects before the outgoing eleventh-grade students went on study leave for their GCE O levels. This gave the new prefects the chance to show their calibre before the summer vacation and before the real thing the following September.

Votes for prefects were cast by all members of the tenth grade, the entire secondary faculty and the outgoing prefects. People made their choices based on the part played by individual students in the life of the school, their leadership qualities, reliability, academic success and participation in school and house teams. As in all years, expectations were high among Debbie's classmates. As in all schools, prefects have prestige and kudos throughout the year.

When the results were announced, there were few surprises. Debbie was relieved and proud to have been elected, but spent more time commiserating with her best friend Tracee Rolle, who failed to win enough votes, than she did celebrating her own achievement.

Assuming the mantle of prefect, doing duties and generally being a role model for the rest of the school was a pleasurable task for Debbie. She slipped into it with the same ease she had shown when she first arrived at the school. 'This was actually the first time I realised that I was a role model, though,' she relates. 'I think we all came to appreciate that that's what we were when we took on the role of prefect. It didn't actually change us, but it made us aware.'

Since those days in May 1992, Debbie has never forgotten that she is a role model for so many young Bahamians, and has constantly lived up to the role in her achievements and her way of life. She knows that she can have a much greater influence now, especially on the lives of Bahamians who struggle as she once did, than she could as a student. She therefore never refuses an opportunity to speak to young Bahamians or try to inspire them to make the most of their talents, and to seek fulfilment and happiness through their own efforts.

Debbie was not quite so successful in the other major event of the semester. The tenth-grade examinations were rigorous and long, and despite studying hard and revising all she could,

Debbie was not prepared for the conveyor belt of tests and papers, sometimes three on the same day. She had never experienced a set of examinations quite so taxing and it served as an unpleasant wake-up call.

Her final grades were even lower than she had feared. She had never imagined that she would slip as low as 2.86, her second semester GPA. She used the average, however, to steel herself, and strengthened her resolve never to do so badly again. She vowed there and then that she would do all she could to ensure that she would graduate with honours and, as in all things she sets her mind to, she began working on improving her situation, in particular her exam technique, straight away.

For St Andrew's students, entering Grade 11 had always marked the beginning of their final year and the ultimate drive towards graduation. For Debbie's grade, however, it was different. The Bahamas had instituted its own national examinations for leaving senior high school students, the Bahamas General Certificate of Secondary Education. The stipulation was that the exams had to be taken by twelfth-grade students. In 1993, when the first exams took place, St Andrew's had no twelfth grade. All students graduated at the end of Grade 11. Debbie's class was to stay an extra year and would become the first mandatory twelfth-graders in the school's history. That meant, of course, that there would be no graduating class in 1993.

Initially, the students in Debbie's year were annoyed at having to stay on an extra year. Many of them had already been at the school since they were four years old and had been expecting to graduate in 1993. 'Why us?' they complained. 'Don't they know we're ready to move on?'

Once they grew accustomed to the idea, however, most thoroughly enjoyed their two years at the top of the school. 'No other students at the school had been prefects for two years, nor had they enjoyed the name of seniors for two years. We came to regard ourselves as special,' is the way they looked at it.

At the beginning of their eleventh grade, the voting took place for the head boy, head girl and their deputies, four coveted positions in the St Andrew's student hierarchy. Again there was a faculty and a student vote. Debbie gained most votes for Deputy Head Girl. She was overjoyed to have gained such a highly desirable position, and realises now that the acceptance and popularity she had felt since her first day there had at that time truly manifested themselves into something real and tangible.

Just a couple of days after the voting, Tommy Robinson drove up to the school's administration offices to speak to Roger Kelty. He had come to ask if Debbie could be given permission to travel to Seoul, the South Korean capital, to represent The Bahamas in the World Junior Track and Field Championships.

He explained that Debbie would catch up with the work and would not use the trip as an excuse for missing any assignments. 'We didn't have to think twice,' says Roger. 'This was such a great opportunity for her that we would never have stood in her way. We knew the kind of student she was and what her work ethic was like. So we all felt positive that she would not only make up the work, but also do us all proud at the games.'

Debbie actually went round to all her teachers before she left and collected a number of assignments. She tried to complete them while she was away, but admits that she did not manage to do very many. There were so many wonderful excursions and events to attend, in addition to watching the races and events in the stadium. She had never been on so long a flight before, and she was fascinated by the experience of the Far East, with its culture, food, music and way of life so different from her own.

There was also the small matter of competing, not just against the best athletes in the Caribbean, but against the best in the world. 'This was a competition on a different scale from anything I had been used to,' Debbie relates. 'We were running in the Olympic Stadium where they held the 1988 Olympics, where Flo-Jo won double gold, and where two of my idols, Merlene Ottey and Gwen Torrence, also ran. Competing there with me were Marion Jones and Ato Bolden, the Trinidadian sprinter. I felt so privileged that I was a bit overawed by the whole thing. I didn't run at my best. I reached the second round of the 100 metres, but could only come in seventh, so I didn't make the semis. I had not been doing any real serious training for about a month before this meet, so I wasn't in my best shape. But it was a great experience, and to have been the only Bahamian selected was a great honour.'

Although it was not a very successful competition for her, Debbie was happy to have felt the atmosphere of a world championship and to have been a part of the intense competition. She returned to Nassau with a bagful of different souvenirs and gifts for friends and teachers, and didn't stop talking about the trip for weeks. Her teachers remember that she caught up with the work long before she stopped talking about her experiences.

A time of contrasts

All this success and positive news from school had to be balanced against what were very difficult times at home. Ms Ferguson was in very poor health and now unable to work at all. There were still candies for sale from the front porch of their tiny wooden house, and she still produced the frozen juices from the freezer that Andrea Lockhart had provided, but some days she felt so unwell that she could not even get up to sell the sweets. This also meant that she was unable to look after any babies during the day, so very little money was coming into the household.

Debbie was very grateful for the lunches and the weekly allowance from Earla Bethel, passed to her by her daughter, Danielle. Debbie managed well to hide the fact that home life was very difficult. She always washed and ironed her own uniform, managing to find enough time between track practices and homework, and she always looked neat and presentable.

Sometimes, however, when she was pumping water in the yard behind the house, she would stop and think. 'What is going on? Here I am, mixing with these very rich kids from their fancy homes with their fancy cars. I'm at the best school in the country and a college place is beckoning. Yet I'm carrying water from a pump and living in a wooden house with one bedroom and no bathroom and no money for anything.' Her normally positive and cheerful attitude would plummet at these thoughts.

Her safety valve was running. When all else seemed bleak and there was no solution to the worries, she would recover her equilibrium with a session at the track, running her heart out and pushing herself to the limit. After satisfying herself and Coach Rahming with her split times and running form in repetitions and practices, she would return home able to face the empty cupboards and the snowy TV screen with just one channel.

Things reached their lowest point at Christmas 1992, when, due to a combination of circumstances that left the Fergusons on their own, Christmas dinner was one that Debbie and her mother have tried hard, but unsuccessfully, to forget. 'I don't know how things got so bad,' Ms Ferguson laments, 'but we really were at rock bottom that Christmas. There was no money for anything. We managed to buy each other a couple of little gifts, but there was nothing left over and all we had for Christmas dinner was a can of spaghetti.'

Debbie knew her friends from St Andrew's would be in their grand houses with their fancy trees surrounded by gifts, while she was in her tiny shack trying to make sense of the situation. They would be enjoying a wonderful turkey dinner with all the trimmings, and she was making do with a can of spaghetti. The unfairness of it all caused her to burst into tears, but Debbie knew she could not afford to wallow in self-pity for long. 'There would have been no point,' she insists. 'That was the reality. I prayed and asked for guidance and pretty soon realised this was just another obstacle or hurdle to be cleared. I felt terrible, but at least I put it in perspective and was able to look ahead. We sat and talked about the things we had to be thankful for and we moved on.'

Ms Ferguson's health deteriorated, however, and surgery was the only option: without it, she would never get well. She did not have medical insurance and the waiting list at Nassau's Princess Margaret Hospital was long, so she took the unusual step of arranging to go back to Jamaica. Through her parents, she could have the surgery there at a fraction of the cost and without the wait.

Although this was the best solution for Ms Ferguson, she did not know what to do about her daughter while she was away. She could not leave her in the house alone: it would not be safe and would cause stress and worry on top of the illness. The date for her departure was fast approaching when Debbie came up with the solution: Ms Lockhart. She had kept in contact with her former sports teacher since leaving Oakes Field School. She knew Ms Lockhart would be pleased to have her and she liked staying at the house with her and the boys. Ms Lockhart agreed readily, so Debbie went to stay while her mother underwent surgery in Jamaica.

Back at school, Debbie focused on her main objective – to reach the honour roll by the end of her eleventh grade – and she threw herself into her studies. Although there were distractions from the Lockhart boys, Thackeray and Labosky, she disciplined herself to ignore the games, TV and fun until after she had finished her homework. Many nights she fell asleep with books open and the light still on, as she tried to study beyond her endurance. 'I was worried about my mom,' explains Debbie, 'and I found the studies took my mind off her and how she might be feeling. Telephone contact was not always the best between Nassau and Jamaica at that time, and sometimes I didn't hear how she was for over a week. I didn't like to ask Ms Lockhart too often if I could use the phone in the house. So I found it better to concentrate on my work. It worked pretty well too.'

As her mother's absence went on, Debbie found staying at the Lockharts more difficult. Ms Lockhart expected her to help out in the house. Debbie had always been used to doing housework, and had no objection to this, but she could not come to terms with the fact that the two boys were not expected to do any. She says, 'I let it get to me after a while. I couldn't accept that I was cleaning and sweeping and they were not asked to do anything. It became one of life's lessons for me. Males are not expected to do certain things, even if the females are overworked and tired out. And that seems to be the way of the world. I vowed then that that would not be the way for me and my husband – I would need a man who would share all the responsibilities and the chores.'

There were other pressing concerns on her mind: the most imminent was the 1993 CARIFTA Games, to be held in Martinique. Debbie was now in the under-20 age group and would be competing against her fellow countrywoman and long-time rival, Savatheda Fynes, later to become one of the Golden Girls relay team.

Debbie's training for the Games received the best of all boosts when her mother called her to tell her that she had been discharged from hospital and could travel home to Nassau. She wasted no time in returning and it was immediately obvious that the surgery had been successful. She was like a new woman: lively and energetic, positive and optimistic. She came back determined to make a fresh start, find a job and move on with her life. So Debbie, who had managed to reconcile her objections to the situation at Ms Lockhart's, returned home with her mother just in time to travel to Martinique with the CARIFTA team.

'It was around this time that I realised just how much I loved travelling,' Debbie reminisces. 'I kept getting these mixed messages in my head. I would look at where I was living and then I would think about Seoul or Cuba or Martinique, and wonder how many other kids, even those kids with plenty of money, had been to those places. I knew I was blessed in many ways: I was at St Andrew's, my benefactors were looking out for me whenever they could – they even paid the rent while my mom was down in Jamaica – and there were teachers there who helped me in many ways. On top of all that, I was given the chance to go to these different countries and see different people and experience different cultures. Yes, I definitely intended to take every possibility where travelling was concerned because I genuinely felt it was opening my mind.'

In 1993, the travelling did not end with the trip to Martinique: in the summer she flew with the Bahamian team to Winnipeg, Canada, for the Pan-American Junior Championships. This was probably the biggest competition she had ever run in. Athletes from all the Americas – North, Central and South – were there. Debbie distinguished herself by winning bronze in the 100 metres final after three gruelling rounds of heats.

Later in the summer, she travelled to Colombia with the senior team, which included Pauline Davis and Savatheda Fynes, for the CAC Senior Championships. Debbie did not compete in any individual events, but was a member of the 4×100-metre relay team. Debbie recaptures her feelings about the summer of 1993: 'It was a high point for me in lots of ways. I had worked hard and done well at school. (She managed the end-of-year exams more successfully and improved her GPA to a respectable 3.30 for the year. More importantly, this was the minimum GPA for entering the honour roll.)

'I still wanted to do better, but I had proved to myself that I could reach the honour's standard. Then there were the international meets I was selected for in countries I had never visited before. I was still pretty young and I found these places so interesting. I guess travelling was really in my blood from that time.'

Debbie was beginning to make a name for herself in many places. She was being recognised by people from all over the region when she went to compete. Her friends in the class would often come to school talking about articles in the newspapers or features in the sports news on Bahamian television that had highlighted Debbie and her achievements of the previous summer.

Debbie, however, was focusing intently on her school work: this was her final year. She had the national exams to take in May and she desperately wanted to graduate with honours. It soon became clear, however, that there was another aspect of school life to be addressed at this stage: college applications and, more specifically, overtures made to her by various universities that were prepared to offer her track scholarships to attend their institutions. Debbie found this something of a distraction, and was happy for the assistance offered by the St Andrew's Guidance Department in coping with the large amounts of reading, and the writing of résumés and personal letters that had to accompany any application.

She also found the reality of thinking about going to university quite difficult. While she knew a college scholarship was a possibility – many people in the track and field set-up had talked to her about it – the reality of going away to study and to run was still a strange concept for her. She had become fully aware of the opportunities that had opened up for her by attending St Andrew's and mixing with students from very different backgrounds to her own. She was, nevertheless, acutely aware of her own situation, and knew that she and her mother could never hope to pay for a college course on their own.

Orinthia Nesbeth, whose influence was never far away from anything that had a direct bearing on the future of her special student, played an important role in selecting the best university for Debbie. She wanted to be sure that Debbie made the right choice. 'I wanted to be sure there would be the right type of support system there for her, wherever she chose. I had become extremely fond of her during the four years of the scholarship. I couldn't think of her going somewhere that wouldn't suit her.'

When the time came to make a choice, there were three serious possibilities: the University of Florida, Rice University and the University of Georgia. A few colleges from California, such as the University of Southern California and the University of California in Los Angeles, had been considered, but Debbie had rejected them because she did not want to be too far away from The Bahamas.

When it came to the final choice, Debbie had to make up her own mind, but Mrs Nesbeth was inclining towards Rice, because it was a smaller, more homely school, with a strong academic reputation. St Andrew's seemed to favour Florida, while Debbie, who wanted to continue to run, but was thinking more about her degree and medical school afterwards, felt divided, because she did not want to upset anyone, least of all Mrs Nesbeth.

There were other important domestic matters to consider too. The famous School Run, which she had missed for two years because her coach thought it would not be advantageous to push herself over a mile while she was concentrating on speed, was looming. She had promised her housemaster that this year she would run. It turned out to be a keen competition between Debbie and Courtney Turtle, who was a year younger than Debbie and a distance specialist, who had been undefeated in School Runs since primary school. The two of them chased each other around the streets surrounding the school and, in the end, Courtney prevailed over Debbie by a mere seven metres.

There was also the inter-house track and field meet, Debbie's last at St Andrew's. Coach Rahming came to watch and supervise his girl's performances; needless to say, she destroyed the opposition. It is interesting, however, that Debbie does not officially hold any St Andrew's records for track and field. The school did not adopt the nickname of The Hurricanes until 1996, when official school records were started again. Debbie actually returned to the school in September 1996 to inaugurate the name of The Hurricanes. At a special ceremony in the school hall, she exhibited her newly won Olympic silver, but also on that day all her achievements in the school colours were destroyed. It is ironic that the name of the school's greatest athlete is nowhere to be seen on the official Hurricanes records table.

In the independent schools track and field meet, Debbie put up one of her greatest performances, gaining 42 of St Andrew's 59 points. 'She seemed irresistible at that meet,' exclaimed her sports teacher. At Easter she travelled again: this time, the CARIFTA

Games were in Barbados. It was another new country for Debbie and another welcome experience. Her love of travelling was growing with every trip. The people she met were stimulating her and continually providing different perspectives and ideas on life. Once again, Debbie performed superbly for her country. She won the 100 metres and came second in the 200, and ran in both the 4×100- and the 4×400-metre relays, in both of which The Bahamas were placed second. Her medal count was growing with each meet and she was regularly achieving personal bests.

When she returned from Barbados, Debbie had to concentrate fully on studying for her national exams. She was taking nine, with a total of 21 different papers, so she had a large amount of studying. The training had to continue alongside her studies because she had been entered for a number of meets in the summer.

Ms Ferguson recalls: 'Debbie's days were long at that time. I used to call her at five in the morning for her morning practice; she went to school for the day and then she was back at the track in the afternoon and evening. She had her work to do when she reached home at about eight or nine. But she was disciplined. She got straight down to her books. Some nights I had to take the books away from her after midnight so she could get some sleep. But she was driven to do well in those exams.' Debbie's desire to make the honour roll never diminished, and she was overjoyed when her efforts in twelfth grade improved her overall GPA to a very impressive 3.61. She did so well in her final year that her ranking in the class for twelfth grade was fifth.

Debbie reasons, 'All those late nights were worth it in the end because I more than achieved my goals. As I tell students now when I'm asked to speak to them, "You have to be prepared to work. You can achieve your goals only if you're prepared to focus and to work." I try to use myself as an example because I did everything I could to get what I wanted – and it worked.'

At graduation, Debbie's whole extended 'family', including Mrs Nesbeth, Mrs Bethel, Mrs Redhead, neighbours and other friends, were there with her mother to witness the occasion. They certainly did not let Debbie forget the evening, giving her the loudest cheers when she walked across the stage to collect her diploma.

'I had plenty of time to get used to the idea of graduating from the best school in the country, but for most people who come from where I do, graduating from St Andrew's was a wild fantasy. I believed it because I lived it, but it still seemed like a dream some of the time,' says Debbie. Describing the occasion is emotional for her, even now.

Tommy Robinson, whose daughter was graduating too, was the guest speaker at the ceremony, and his speech could well have been about Debbie. He spoke about the 'Cs' and the 'Ds' of character: 'competitiveness', 'contributions', 'determination', 'discipline', 'dedication', and, most important, 'desire'. Certainly, Debbie had exemplified all six in her four years at St Andrew's. She continues to demonstrate these to the world as she extends her career and develops her interests in life in general.

When the graduation celebrations were over and Debbie had danced the night away with George and her other friends at the prom, there were two important international meets to prepare for that summer: her second visit to the World Junior Championships, held in Lisbon, Portugal, and her first exposure to the Commonwealth Games, hosted by the city of Victoria in Canada. In Portugal, another new country for her, Debbie reached the finals of both the 100 metres and the 200 metres, finishing fifth in the former and fourth in the latter.

In the Commonwealth Games, running against senior athletes from all over the British Commonwealth, she reached the semi-final of the 200 metres and ran the lead-off leg in the 4×100-metre relay, helping the team to finish a creditable fifth.

Debbie admits to being overawed by the size and scale of these games. She was just 18, had just finished high school, and was running against great athletes of whom she had only heard, such as Cathy Freeman from Australia. The experience served as very worthwhile preparation for the more important competitions to come in the years ahead.

It was actually an experience off the track that Debbie remembers most about the Games in Victoria. Each participating country was invited to send an athlete to the formal banquet, to be held on the eve of the competition and attended by officials and diplomats from all the Commonwealth countries and members of the organising committee. Understandably, no one in The Bahamas contingent was willing to go, preferring to rest and prepare for the competition. Debbie, young, eager to please and ready for any new experience, said she would fill the empty seat. And what a seat it was.

When she arrived, she was directed to her place at one of the large round tables, where each place setting seemed to have more knives and forks than she had in her entire cutlery box. She had no sooner sat down and started to survey the packed ballroom when everyone stood formally. The room was filled with the sounds of a fanfare introducing the guest of honour. Who would this guest of honour be? None other than Queen Elizabeth II, the leader of the British Commonwealth. And where did she sit? Nowhere else but the empty place next to Debbie.

Debbie had hardly managed to quell the pounding in her heart before one of the other people at the table introduced her to The

Queen. Debbie had never been more relieved that her good manners and politeness are absolutely natural and come spontaneously. She simply said, 'Good evening, ma'am,' without even thinking, while her nerves jangled and she tried to loosen her tongue in case she was asked to say anything else.

Thus, as another era of her rapidly accelerating life came to a close, Debbie was left to relish the many opportunities that were beginning to come her way. She looked forward to the great challenge of university and the even greater opportunities that it would present. She felt prepared and confident, although nothing could have actually prepared her for the demands that she would face in just a few months, during her first year at college.

CHAPTER 4
A GEORGIA BULLDOG

Freshman year: ups and downs

The summer of 1994 was one of transition for Debbie. She was packing up her books, files and personal documents, and preparing to leave the familiar surroundings of Nassau and The Bahamas to move to a new world at the university she had eventually chosen.

Contrary to the ideas of her St Andrew's guidance counsellor and Mrs Nesbeth, her benefactor, Debbie had chosen to go to the University of Georgia, in Athens in the US. She was going to take up a full track and field scholarship and begin the long journey towards realising her ambition of becoming a paediatrician.

While she admits that she had little idea of what was in store for her, she had been to Athens before on a familiarisation visit while still at St Andrew's. During the short flight from Nassau, she was able to picture the red brick college buildings and their surroundings in the valley below the downtown area, and imagine herself on the track at the Bulldogs' stadium, where she hoped to achieve great things. She would also have the company of at least one familiar face: her good friend and fellow CARIFTA teammate, Tonique Williams, was also beginning her college career in Georgia at the same time.

In spite of the track scholarship, Debbie's thoughts were not strongly focused on athletics. She saw this scholarship as an opportunity to do something she had often dreamed about, but little believed that she would ever realise: go to medical school and become a doctor, specialising in treating children. Her eyes had been opened to the possibilities while attending St Andrew's, but as a teenager running Saturday errands for the Caribbean Bottling Company for pocket money, the dream had remained just that – until the scouts began to show an interest in luring her to their respective colleges.

She still regarded the track, however, as a means to fulfil her real ambition. She entered the University of Georgia as a student who wanted to be a doctor first and a track athlete second. She genuinely loved the running, but uppermost in her mind was the thought of becoming Doctor Debbie Ferguson, paediatrician. Representing The Bahamas at the Olympics was a distant second.

On the flight she recalled the familiarisation visit. She had been assigned a buddy, a hostess whose task was to show Debbie around and introduce her to some of the aspects of student life at Georgia. The buddy had focused almost exclusively on one aspect of college life: the parties and the opportunities for developing your social life.

To be fair, everyone who attends the University of Georgia comments on its fantastic social life: everything that exists in Athens is there because of, and to serve, the students of the university. Athens is the university, and the bars, coffee shops and restaurants are all within the confines of the college campus.

This emphasis on social life and the activities after lectures almost caused Debbie to turn her back on the University of Georgia and look more seriously at her second choice, Rice University in Houston, Texas, which she believed would be better preparation for a medical career. Even now, as a teenager just about to experience the freedom of living away from home for the first time, she was not interested in parties. She had a mature and level outlook that led her to fix her goals and ambitions clearly and sensibly. She attributes this level-headedness to her background and upbringing: she wanted to study and achieve; she was accustomed to training her body for the track, not abusing it with late nights, alcohol and over-indulgence.

She had almost decided on Rice, but she did want to run track as well, and she knew that Georgia offered her better athletics opportunities. There was also the presence of Coach Norbert Elliott, a Bahamian Olympian, at Georgia, and the personal visit he had paid Debbie and her mother earlier in 1994. These two factors eventually persuaded her to abide by her original choice.

Her Nassau coach, Pancho Rahming, also stepped in. Debbie had been training under his watchful eye since she was 10 and, as in most things, she went to her surrogate father for advice. He had spoken very highly of Coach Elliott and advised her to go to Georgia. This, coupled with Debbie's explicit respect for Rahming's opinions and Elliott's own personality – he himself had been very friendly and genuine when he visited – persuaded Debbie's mother that he was a man she could trust with Debbie's future prospects. This finally swayed her in favour of Georgia.

The University of Georgia had other advantages: one of them was its campus. Debbie loved it from the moment she first set eyes on it. The fact that the school was the town and the town was the school, and that Athens had grown because the university had grown, made it ideal for Debbie's purposes. She believed there would be fewer distractions than in a college situated in a city like Atlanta – and Debbie did not want distractions.

Nevertheless, Georgia is a large school with a diverse student population. Debbie knew this would be a challenge, but she also saw it as an advantage because it would provide competition. She had grown up on competition; she thrived on it and she knew that at Georgia, both on the track and in the lecture halls, it would be keen and tough. She felt ready, however: she had never shirked a challenge and felt she could face it, and succeed.

She felt a great excitement as she anticipated the next four years; excitement and a great sense of gratitude. She felt blessed and grew more and more convinced that someone was looking out for her: the possibilities were increasing with each new opportunity. Debbie felt humbled and asked herself, 'Why me? Of all the kids in The Bahamas to be given the chance to go to St Andrew's, it was me! So I did track; sure, I enjoyed it, but I did track because I liked it and now, all of a sudden I've been given a scholarship to go to the school of my choice, so I reckon somebody has got to be looking out for me.'

Alongside these thoughts, by way of explaining what she saw as amazing good fortune, were ideas that her path had somehow already been written. This was her destiny. It was up to her to fulfil that destiny and follow the predestined route, which to her meant really making the most of it. As her grandmother had taught her from the biblical parable, 'Make the most of your talent.' Her impoverished childhood and the hard times growing up meant that she had never dreamt of going to college: she would never have been able to afford it. Yet here she was about to step into a very good American university on a full scholarship. Debbie pinched herself on numerous occasions to make sure she was not the main character in a fairy tale.

Although her familiarisation visit had shown her a side of college life for which she was totally unprepared, she still somewhat naively believed that all students went to college to study hard: certainly this was how she approached college. She therefore received a sharp awakening when she came into direct contact with the kind of distractions that college life places in the way

100

of unsuspecting freshmen. Of course, she was tempted. Offers to attend the party of the century or to go to this dance and that other function were occasionally too difficult to resist, but Debbie never let these distractions divert her from her chosen way. 'I have one chance,' she reasoned with herself, 'and I'm not about to blow it.'

Remarkably mature given the circumstances, Debbie pledged to combat the peer pressure and really make something of herself while at university. This was partly out of respect for the person she knew herself to be, but also for those people whom she regarded as her godparents: those kind and supportive people in The Bahamas who had been so instrumental in providing her with the prospects of making her once impossible dream come true. Debbie puts it quite simply: 'The parties went out of the window!'

This would have been a difficult decision for some, but for Debbie it was not only easy, but essential. And it was not unusual for her to give up playing and partying so that she could study. She had been doing this in every school she had attended. Given the level of fitness she needed to maintain to cope with her training regimen, there was really no other choice. While her friends and other freshmen were out partying after classes, Debbie had to go to training sessions and then prepare for the next day's classes. Consequently, she quickly realised that to keep up with the others who had those extra hours for their books, whether they used them or not, she had to work long into the night. She also insisted on making the most of the study time she could find.

At Georgia there was a compulsory two-hour study hall for freshmen students and Debbie duly went along. Ironically, this study hall proved to be one of the major distractions that she faced. The majority of the students did not go there to study: as far as Debbie could make out, they attended for any reason except study. Some would be listening to music, others would be chatting, telling jokes or laughing, and others used it as a time to arrange their already crowded social lives.

Debbie quickly realised that study hall was more of a handicap than an advantage and she pledged to do something about it. She went to the authorities and asked if she could be excused from the noise and demotivating atmosphere created by football and basketball players and be given permission to work in her room or in the library.

Her request was not accepted instantly, but the authorities did listen to her and she pleaded her case strongly, urgently, and, in the end, persuasively. Eventually, she was given sole permission to work away from the other students. There was one condition, one that she had little trouble in meeting: she had to keep her grades up.

Debbie still thinks that the special dispensation over study hall only applied to her because she proved to the authorities that she would maintain her GPA and meet all her deadlines. They did not have to monitor her – her self-motivation was enough. It immediately became clear to the authorities that this was not a student trying to skip study time, because she actually wished she had more time for her books.

Of course, the main reason that Debbie had to make the most of every spare moment for studying was because of the amount of time that she had to spend training. The hours she had spent at the Thomas A. Robinson National Stadium in the evenings and at the weekends with Pancho Rahming had prepared her in many ways. She quickly realised, however, that now she was working in a different league: more time was necessary and more was expected of her.

Her new coach, fellow Bahamian Norbert Elliott, who had been highly recommended by Rahming, immediately took Debbie under his wing. He devised a training regimen specifically designed for his new charge, which placed much more emphasis on weights and strength work, aspects of training she had rarely explored before. Debbie surprised herself with the improvement that she recorded during her first year in Georgia, and gives all the credit to Elliott's methods and training programme. She arrived with a 100-metre personal best of 11.48 seconds, the fastest in the world for a schoolgirl. This she lowered to 11.19 before the end of that year: a time that broke Gwen Torrence's long-standing college record. Debbie did not feel that she was running very consistently, but her speed had certainly increased. She was astonished to have achieved this new Georgia record in her first year.

The relationship between athlete and coach is very special. Debbie's relationship with the only coach she had known prior to moving to Georgia was that of father and daughter. Debbie trusted Pancho Rahming in everything, believed in him and would do anything for him. She brought that same open, trusting attitude to Coach Elliott, and there was an immediate rapport between. She put herself into his hands completely and he led her to achieve levels of performance that she would not have believed possible in such a short time.

For most of that first year, they spent hours and hours together on the track – Debbie running and Elliott observing; Elliott talking and instructing, and Debbie listening; Debbie stretching and Elliott explaining. He would invite her to have dinner on Sundays with his wife and three children, and even picked her up from Atlanta airport and drove her back to Athens when she had been away or home to The Bahamas.

Debbie could feel new strength and speed developing as her physical potential grew. Elliott was creating the right environment for learning to take place and motivating his new student athlete in exactly the right way. Of course, Debbie was already very highly motivated, but Elliott had a way of ensuring that her motivation never waned. He maintained Debbie's excitement and enthusiasm for training and improving her form.

A good coach fulfils many roles and Elliott seemed ideally suited to play all that were required of him. He communicated well with Debbie, who had little difficulty in understanding his demands or putting them into practice. He set realistic goals which pushed her and tested her, but which she felt were within her capabilities. He monitored her training sessions meticulously. He advised her on nutrition. He facilitated, counselled and organised. He acted as chauffeur. He answered Debbie's doubts and he reassured her when she despaired of achieving a time or completing a set of repetitions.

As well as developing the runner athletically, the coach plays a critical role in personal development through the protracted time they spend together. There is without doubt an inherent power imbalance that coaches must be careful not to exploit in a negative way. Athletes take their advice seriously and are easily susceptible to poor advice or unreasonable demands.

The Elliott–Ferguson relationship was ideal for much of Debbie's freshman year, but towards the end of the second semester she began to detect a subtle change. She cannot put her finger on any one moment when she first became aware that something was amiss, but it was as if an invisible presence was lurking in the background. For most of the track season, however, she was able to remain focused and put to the back of her mind the strangeness that had developed in her relationship with her coach. There was, however, another aspect of being a member of the college track team that contributed to the stresses she was already feeling: the travelling.

There were weekly meets which involved travelling to other colleges and distant venues, all of which ate into Debbie's study and work time. For a while during her first year, she really wondered if she could meet all the demands that she felt were placed upon her, especially when, even with her outstanding work ethic, she found herself struggling to keep up.

Everything she had to deal with began, slowly and inexorably, to take its toll on her mental health. When her grandfather died in Jamaica during that first year, she had to seek counselling in order to find calm and rediscover her equilibrium. This was a man whom she had admired and looked up to. It was he who had provided the positive model for her attitude to work, and he who had been blessed with a character founded on humility and respect for his fellow human beings. Debbie has always tried to emulate these positive attributes of her grandfather.

The news of his death did not reach her until the day before the funeral. She desperately wanted to attend the service, but did not know if she would be able to get a flight. There was also the considerable problem of finding the money for the ticket. She eventually borrowed the money and caught the bus to Atlanta airport.

By the time she arrived, the flight to Kingston had already departed, so she had to wait until the following day. By the time she arrived in Little London, the funeral had taken place and her grandfather had been laid to rest in the field behind his house. Disappointed and obviously upset, Debbie went through the motions with her family, grieving for her lost role model. But she never felt a sense of completion and was left dissatisfied and frustrated at not having paid her final respects at the funeral with the other members of the family.

It was, however, a very different experience that had the most profound effect on her during her freshman year. For some time, the experience fundamentally altered her feelings about the school.

Debbie found her first-year maths class a considerable challenge and she struggled to make even moderate grades. This in itself was a new experience for her, as she had always been fairly competent in the subject and had eventually done quite well at St Andrew's. She was advised to take some extra classes.

After one of these extra classes, she decided to wait behind to ask the lecturer for clarification on a particular procedure that she was finding very difficult. 'He took me to one side and began to explain, but then, to my horror, I felt his hand move over my body and touch my breasts.' It was not an accident, not a chance or passing graze, but a deliberate sexual advance. 'I was in shock and I did not know what to do. This was a deliberate molestation,' she explains. Unable to think, she felt stunned, angry and bitterly disappointed. She tries to explain how she felt about the incident: 'I trusted the man as I had always trusted all my teachers. I had taken the trouble to arrange to stay behind to clarify in my mind something that was troubling me regarding a certain maths problem, and this is how he treated me. I did not know what to do, but dealt with it initially in the only way I thought I could, and that was by not saying anything about it to anyone.'

Debbie was alone in what was still a strange place and had none of her support group anywhere near. She felt exposed. She did not know how others would react if she mentioned it. So she retreated into herself and remained silent.

It did, however, affect her approach and attitude to the class. She would attend, but in body only, her mind anywhere but on the man presenting the topics. She had always sat eagerly in the front, but now she would slink in at the back and pay little or no attention.

She started to do badly in the class and her grades began to drop. She contemplated dropping out of school. She was stressed, and the whole experience and its aftermath were clearly detrimental to an 18-year-old living away from home for the first time. She had never imagined anything like this happening to her in her first year at college.

Clearly something had to be done if she were not to fail her first-year maths class. Eventually, she went to Coach Elliott and told him what had happened. He informed the athletic adviser, who recommended that Debbie switch maths classes, and it was then that action was taken.

She was transferred to another section of the maths class with a female professor. The transformation was almost instantaneous. Debbie progressed from an unhappy student going through the motions and on the verge of failing, to the vibrant, enthusiastic young woman determined to succeed and occupy the top place in the class she had had before the incident. The new professor was understanding and supportive and Debbie responded to her positively. She felt comfortable again and refocused herself on her ultimate goals.

The incident had not passed completely, however, because another female student was sexually harassed by the same professor. Debbie's earlier complaint had been placed on file and she was asked to testify against him in support of charges brought by the second girl. Debbie was pleased to be able to give this support and delighted when the other female student won the case. The professor was removed surreptitiously from the faculty. Everything was arranged discreetly to avoid a scandal, but the professor was not seen again. The whole incident quickly became an unpleasant memory locked away.

Fortunately, Debbie did not find that these events distracted her from training. She continued to train hard. The more Coach Elliott tried to control her, however, the more she started to assert her own personality and ideas. There were so many factors to take into account. She was still a relatively new girl. She was on a full track scholarship. He was her personal coach. She had to work with him and she needed him professionally.

She toyed with the idea of telling one of the other coaches about her unease with their relationship, but she did not know how they would take it, nor did she have any idea how to explain it. She contemplated leaving the university altogether and spoke about it to her boyfriend George, then in Nassau. He could not understand why she was becoming so upset and convinced her to stay and try to work things out.

'This was her one chance,' he reasoned. 'She had to try to stay focused and not let anything cause her to slip. I had to be hard with her really, but I didn't want her to give it all up.'

In spite of this, Debbie knew that she had to do something: she felt that she was losing her identity and her self-esteem. Even given the new-found strength and speed, she was beginning to lose faith in herself, that essential quality that all athletes need to succeed at the highest level.

Eventually, she came up with a plan and was courageous enough to put it into action. She told herself that she was responsible for at least 50 per cent of her successes, that it was she who was actually doing the running, and that she was a person and an athlete in her own right, with a God-given talent. She would show Coach Elliott by deciding herself what training she would take part in, what repetitions she would run and what split times she would aim for.

To put it directly, Debbie became rebellious – not in a negative way, because she knew what she had to do in order to maintain her standards and set new ones for herself. She used the track as a way to escape from the psychological turmoil. Her desire to rid herself of what she saw as her coach's dominance and control motivated her to push herself harder than she ever had before. This method of coping underlined Debbie's fierce determination and confidence in herself, and emphasised once again her clear and accurate focus on aspects of her life that are the most important.

The success of her new approach became clear when the track season opened in January 1995 with an indoor meet at the Clemson Invitational. Debbie burst out of the blocks for the 55-metre dash and won her first race as a Georgia Bulldog in the stunning time of 6.89 seconds. Not only did she come first, but she reached the NCAA qualifying time in her initial collegiate race. At the time, she was unaware of what she had achieved and remembers reacting to her coaches' enthusiastic reception with a shrug, albeit a satisfied one, and little more.

The University of Georgia competes in the SEC (South Eastern Conference of College Sports), and after the Clemson meet Debbie won SEC Indoor Championships in the 55- and 200-metre dashes, thoroughly enjoying her first experiences of indoor racing. She also had strong performances in the 55 and 200 metres at the Indoor NCAA Championships, finishing third in both events.

Coming between the indoor and outdoor seasons at Georgia were the CARIFTA Games in the Cayman Islands. These were held over the Easter weekend in 1995 and Debbie was due to represent The Bahamas in the 100 metres, 200 metres, the 4×100- and 4×400 metre relays. These were to be her sixth and last CARIFTA Games. It was fitting that they should be staged in Cayman because it was there, in 1989, that she had made her first appearance on foreign soil in

109

the Central American and Caribbean Junior Championships. Then she had won the overall title and caused the region to take notice of this new youngster from The Bahamas. Six years later, she would be running in the same stadium and hoping for a similar result.

Flying down to Cayman, she was relaxed, but focused. The tensions that had begun to appear between her and Coach Elliott were forgotten for a few days and she was able concentrate on the races. Elliott was not there in Cayman, but her mother was, along with many other coaches and friends from Nassau.

The Cayman Islands government had refurbished the track and field stadium for these games. It looked magnificent in the bright, early April sunshine for the daytime events and under new floodlights for the evenings. Debbie won her way through to the finals in both individual events without difficulty, although the local favourite, Cydonie Mothersille, beat her into second place in the semi-final of the 100. This was just a minor hiccup: in both finals she won gold, with something to spare. Her new strength and speed were highly impressive and she maintained her form and focus in the 4×100-metre relay, in which The Bahamas also won gold.

The final event of the games was the 4×400-metre relay. Debbie was feeling understandably weary after the heats and finals of the other events. This was to be a fitting ending to the championships. It was close for the first two legs, but the third leg was disastrous for The Bahamas: the runner lost contact with the leaders and handed over the baton to Debbie about 30 metres behind Jamaica, then leading.

Debbie set her jaw determinedly, took the baton and began to run down the leading athlete. She continued to gain, until along the back straight the distance between them was a mere 5 metres. As they came on to the last curve it looked as if Debbie was on the

Jamaican's shoulder. They matched each other stride for stride, Debbie calling on reserves of energy that she did not know she had.

Into the home stretch Debbie had given her all, and her opponent, a 400-metre specialist, began to edge a little further into the lead. Still Debbie surged again, but she simply did not have quite enough reserves left and her superhuman effort was not sufficient. Debbie had caught up 25 metres, but even her determination and desire were unable to make up the rest, and Jamaica held on to take the gold, by just 5 metres. As always, Debbie was the first to congratulate the athlete who had beaten her, but she admits that the hug she gave her was as much to keep from falling over as to say 'Well done'.

When the games were over, there was only one possible candidate for the coveted Austin Sealy Award for the outstanding athlete of the games. Debbie accepted the accolade with gratitude and pride. 'This was definitely an honour,' she says, 'and it felt great to end my junior career in the place where it had really begun in such a superb way. I felt I had done well all through my CARIFTA career, so this was really an honour.' Debbie left Cayman a double individual champion, proud, relaxed and successful, determined to cope with the stresses of life on the Georgia Bulldogs track team.

When the weather became warmer and the outdoor season began, Debbie's stream of success continued: in the SEC Outdoor Championships, she finished third in both the 100- and 200-metre dashes, as well as being part of the third-placed 4×400-metre relay team and the fifth-placed 4×100-metre team. In all, she rounded up 14.5 points in her first SEC Outdoor Championships, to help Georgia to its first and only SEC Championship in the history of the women's programme.

She finished third in the 100- and 200-metre dashes at the Outdoor NCAA Championships, as well as fourth as part of the

111

4×100-metre team. With the help of the 13.25 points she earned in her first NCAA Outdoor Championships, Georgia recorded a third-place finish with 41.3 points. That record still stands as the Lady Bulldogs' best outdoor finish.

In total, Debbie ended her freshman year with the University of Georgia with five All-American honours, accomplishments that far exceeded her wildest dreams. The achievement of that freshman year that she treasures most, however, was breaking Gwen Torrence's University of Georgia record for the 100 metres. Torrence had been one of Debbie's heroines. A gold medallist at the Barcelona Olympics, she had inspired the 16-year-old who had watched the race on television at home in Nassau. Now she had already superseded her in the 100 metres, and was setting her sights on her 200-metre record as well.

These results also demonstrated to Debbie that she actually had some real track talent. She had beaten girls who had beaten her in the Junior World Championships and she felt she could do even better. 'You can do this!' she continually told herself. 'I have no idea what is going to happen as far as my coach is concerned, but just stay focused and you could really achieve something on the track.'

Chance meetings

Debbie's second year, her sophomore, was much less stressful. Nothing happened to distract her from her studies and her training progressed smoothly. Her relationship with Coach Elliott was no better, but they tolerated each other most of the time. Elliott was still recognised as her coach, but little remained of the coach–athlete relationship. Debbie was becoming more and more responsible for her own training regimen.

Academically, even though she found the content of the lectures tougher, she maintained her grades. She kept up with the workload and had little difficulty fitting in everything that made demands on her time. Dorian Roach, an old school friend from St Andrew's who was one year ahead of her at Georgia, remembers that he and his roommate would often try to persuade Debbie to join them for concerts or dances, or just at one of the bars downtown, but Debbie, as graciously as she could, always refused, determined not to let herself be sidetracked or distracted from her studies. Dorian remembers that she was well known around the university for her dedication to her studies and was universally admired for her single-mindedness and purpose.

When the 1996 track season opened, Debbie was relaxed and showed no signs of slipping as she took her first NCAA title in the indoor 200 metres. She also finished second in the 55 metres, both improvements on the performances of her freshman year. Georgia finished in second place in the team, scoring 34 points at the NCAA Indoor Championships, the best finish in school history. Debbie's contribution to the points total was, of course, significant.

Later in the season at the NCAA Outdoor Championships, Debbie finished fourth in the 100-metre dash, fifth in the 200-metre dash and fifth as part of the 400-metre relay team. These results were not as good as her first year and she was a little disappointed. She recognised that she had not accomplished what she wanted, to improve on her performances of the previous year, but she told herself that this was the toughest college competition in the world and she was still there with the best of them. She also took comfort from the fact that by the end of her first two seasons in Athens she had already claimed 10 All-American honours, only two short of the record held by her Bulldog predecessor, Gwen Torrence.

Later in 1996, Debbie joined her Bahamian teammates in Atlanta for the Olympic Games, and crowned an amazing two years by winning silver in the 4×100-metre relay. This achievement is covered in more detail in Chapter 5.

Towards the end of Debbie's sophomore year, the next intake of students came on their familiarisation visit. Debbie was asked to show around a young recipient of a track scholarship like herself. She was called Sharkara Grant and there were more similarities between them than just the track scholarship. Sharkara had also grown up in Jamaica. She and Debbie became instant friends and when Sharkara eventually started her career at Georgia, she and Debbie did many things together. When they finally competed together on the Bulldogs' team, they became roommates and were inseparable on journeys to other colleges for meets.

Debbie remembers, 'Sharkara and I hit it off from the beginning. We would talk and laugh and enjoy ourselves all the time. She has told me on more than one occasion that it was my influence during her familiarisation visit that persuaded her to come to Georgia. One day, on a flight back from Boise [Idaho], we were in different rows on the plane. She was two rows in front of me and there was a German family in the row between us. We carried on our conversation over the family's heads and they seemed fascinated by our chatter. Finally, they offered to move so we could sit next to each other, but they were so nice and spoke such good English that I ended up talking to them far more than I talked to Sharkara. They were called Steyskal. That day on the plane I met Frau Angelika and her daughters Corinna and Kirsten.

'They were so interested in me and my running. I found them so likeable that we swapped numbers and addresses. We have kept in touch ever since. They have visited The Bahamas with Gunter, Frau Angelika's husband – they came for Christmas 2002. I have stayed with them at least once each year while I've been on the European tour. They treat me like a princess when I am there with them and nothing is too much trouble.

'When we were training in Herzogenaurach, their home town, before the Athens Olympics, they chauffeured anyone in the team wherever they needed to go and threw a small dinner party for all of us before we left.

'Corinna, the older of the girls, and I became very close. We made a bond that when we had kids of our own we would do an exchange programme. Her kids would come to The Bahamas and mine would go to Germany. In that way, the children would learn a foreign language by being immersed in it and also come to experience a different culture.

'I believe kids need as much exposure to different stimuli as they can get, as early as they can get it. The Steyskals actually live in the town where Adidas equipment is made. It was quite a coincidence, because Adidas became my shoe sponsor. I had to visit the town to fulfil the agreements of the sponsorship. I could visit the family at the same time.'

Chance and coincidence perhaps, but it is an example of Debbie's belief that great things can come from small, unlikely beginnings, and that it is important to talk to everyone sincerely: no one is uninteresting and everyone can add positively to our experiences.

Debbie was impatient for the 1997 season, but, as she prepared for it, she realised that something was causing a serious change in her approach to life. She was now thinking of herself as an athlete first and a student second. This, of course, meant that the possibilities of a track career and becoming a professional athlete were beginning to replace the original intention of becoming a paediatrician.

When Debbie first realised this, she was a little alarmed. When she thought further and contemplated the effect this change of heart might have on those who had sponsored her and supported her since she went to St Andrew's, she felt guilty: she knew they all firmly believed that track is an ephemeral career compared to medicine. It is so short-lived that they thought she should regard running as a diversion that must not detract from the real work of university: achieving a degree and preparing the way for medical school.

She also felt some twinges of guilt because she was going back on her own word and, in some ways, letting herself down. These feelings of uncertainty and guilt were to play a part for the rest of her time at Georgia. They did not recede until The Bahamas women's relay team won gold in Sydney. Not until that moment in 2000 did her decision to follow her dreams onto the track rather than into a hospital seem vindicated, and she was able to shed the guilt and feel truly comfortable about being a professional athlete.

Red-shirt year

As mentioned, Debbie's Olympic achievements are covered in the following chapter. We will see then how successful she was in Atlanta in 1996. As she prepared for the 1997 college season, she was encouraged by her Olympic success and determined to build on her achievements on the world stage and carry these over to the SEC and NCAA Championships: she wanted to make a statement and come out on top. She began her off-season training, preparing for the competition ahead, but nothing could have prepared her for what happened during the fall of her junior year.

Debbie describes it like this: 'I'm training. I'm running and all of a sudden I'm not moving. I'm running round the track and there are freshmen who are not even on scholarship, kids who wouldn't normally come within 10 metres of me, overtaking me, beating me.'

Debbie could not understand what was happening. She was feeling no pain. In fact, her body felt fine, but she just could not move in the way she wanted. She asked her legs for that extra effort and expected them to respond in the way they always had, but nothing was forthcoming. It was as if the tank was empty.

She also noticed weakness when she was lifting weights. She would be down for a squat lift, start to rise, and suddenly lack of strength meant that she would have to complete the lift almost on one leg. Nothing she did led to any improvement. She rested, she did more stretches, she used all kinds of rubs and lotions, but nothing had any effect. So began the long, tedious rounds of going to doctors, visiting specialists, taking X-rays, undergoing MRIs in Athens, Atlanta and surrounding regions, and suffering the double disappointments of not diagnosing the cause and seeing no improvement in her running.

'Why can't I run?' she lamented. 'And why can't any of these experts tell me what's wrong?' Some thought the slight discomfort she felt in her lower back was the cause, but all the tests were negative. Some thought there was pressure on her sacrum (the triangular bone between the hip bones and the pelvis), but it was generally assumed that if this were the case, she would not be able to run at all.

Debbie was naturally depressed and disappointed by this loss of form and felt acute frustration that not even specialists could diagnose the problem. She began to wonder if this was the end of her track achievements. Had fate, up to now so good to her, decided to play a spiteful trick and deprive her of the rest of her career?

In desperation she turned to a neurologist and chiropractor, Dr Natalia Kogan. She eventually provided an explanation, and traced the cause back to the head injury she had received when she fell as a child.

Natalia Kogan discovered that there had been some damage to the right side of the brain as a result of the trauma. This in turn had produced some inconsistencies in the neurological network of the left side. This was causing a weakness in the leg. It had never manifested itself before, but now, possibly as a result of the years of training and competing, it had, and had caused this distressing loss of form.

Although the diagnosis seemed plausible, treating the problem was difficult. Meditation and yoga were tried with equal enthusiasm – Debbie would have tried anything, so desperate was she to regain her form and speed – but neither proved effective. In a final attempt to cure the problem, beams of light stimuli were used in an attempt to invigorate the right side of her brain. Again, Debbie attended the treatment positively, but remained depressed at the lack of any immediate response.

She was still plagued with doubts about her ability ever to run again. She was also tortured by another worry: she might even lose her scholarship. This was too dreadful to contemplate, because without it there was no way she could continue at college.

It seemed to Debbie at this time that the world was caving in. 'No more track,' she thought, 'because no one can tell me why I can't run fast any more, and no more dreams of being a doctor because I won't be able to pay for the school.'

She was at her lowest ebb since going to Georgia, lower even than she had been in the freshman maths class. Athletes whom she had beaten as a matter of course the previous year were now beating her hands down. The coaches had been watching the decline in Debbie's performance and could not believe what they were seeing. They tried to encourage her, but eventually took the only logical decision possible, to have Debbie 'red-shirt' her junior year. This meant that she would not compete for that season, but would continue to study and complete courses. It also meant that she would still have two more seasons to compete. (NCAA rules state that a student can only compete for four years.)

The coaches feared she would only be a shadow of her real self if she ran for the Bulldogs in 1997, so they withdrew her from competition and saved her from a wasted year of competing. She would have an extra year at the college, making five years, while only competing for four. Of course, it was not quite as straightforward as that because there was the question of the scholarship.

Debbie feared that the University would not be happy with one of their scholarship athletes doing nothing for a year. She did not know if they would pay for her courses for a fifth year. The parties concerned met and explained everything to her. Much to her relief, they told her that although she would 'red-shirt' her junior year, the scholarship would continue into an extra year. They added that they were confident that a solution to the physical problem would be found.

Once this decision had been made, Debbie was given time off from training, and she rested. She found this frustrating, but at least it gave her extra time to focus on her studies. On the positive side, the extra year of attendance meant that she could space out the academic courses to a certain extent, and this, in its own way, reduced the pressure. It made fulfilling the graduation requirements a little easier.

During the second semester she began doing some light workouts: she felt that she just could not take the whole year off from training. Slowly, almost imperceptibly, she felt the strength returning to her legs and something like the old spring in her stride. Gradually, she regained her speed and started to beat the girls who had overtaken her earlier in the year.

Her recovery was complete when, in June 1997, she made the qualifying time in the Bahamas National Championships, and in the summer went with The Bahamas team to the IAAF World Championships in Athens, Greece. She approached the Championships nervously, because she had not run enough competitive races during the season and did not feel her usual will to win as she ran.

'I was not in top shape for racing,' Debbie explains. 'I had rediscovered my speed, but that competitive instinct had not returned. As a result, I felt pleased with my 100 metres progress. I made it through to the semi-final and felt comfortable all the way. But that semi-final was tough and I couldn't find the power to go any further.'

Debbie has always thrived on racing, and her time in Athens in 1997 proves that a sprinter needs race experience before a protracted tournament like the 100 metres in the World Championships. 'In a one-off race, my injury lay-off probably wouldn't have had very much effect, but in a series of races like this it was very important,' Debbie says. Her great friend and roommate, Savatheda Fynes, won her way through to the 100-metre final and, in what was a personal best at that time, won the bronze. Another Bahamian, Eldece Clarke, had also been in the semi-final of the 100 metres, so Bahamian hopes were high for the 4×100-metre relay. Pauline Davis completed the team with Debbie, Eldece and Savatheda. The Bahamian women were clearly a unit to be feared, and when they won their semi-final in just two-tenths of a second slower than the United States in the other semi-final, many were tipping the Bahamians to take gold. But something went very wrong in the final.

Debbie's memory of the race is very blurred, such is the disappointment she still feels. She describes the event: 'We were definitely one of the favourites. We were all running well at the time, but hearing people tell us we could beat the Americans went to the heads of a couple of the team. They started thinking more about the money we were going to win than about the race itself.

'I remember on the practice track before the race a full-scale argument started over how to spend the prize money. We hadn't even run the race yet! This was not the way to prepare for a World Championship final. We were really not in any frame of mind to run when we went out on to the track.'

Consequently, the women ran half a second slower than they had in the semi-final and finished a disappointing sixth. Debbie's blurred memory of the race recalls the baton not even making it around the track. The team did finish, but a multitude of recriminations included blame for Debbie's inefficient handling of the baton.

'I honestly can't remember too much about it all,' she says, 'because the disappointment was so hurtful. I don't understand what made us act the way we did, but it obviously affected us as a team and we paid the price. I told myself at that time that we had to learn from this and not let ourselves get distracted from the main business in the future and keep our focus on the running.'

The injury is still a mystery. No one has successfully diagnosed the cause, but Debbie is of course grateful that she overcame it. She still suffers from stiffness in the lower back area, especially in the off-season when she is concentrating on weights. She finds it strange that it never troubles her during the track season and believes that stretching and running are actually beneficial. Long flights sometimes cause it to flare up, but never to the degree of 1997, and any other injuries she has suffered have not been directly connected.

Plaudits and titles: farewell to Georgia

After the disheartening experience of her junior year, Debbie approached the next year determined to erase the memory and scale new heights on the track. Not even her wildest fantasies, however, could have prepared her for the successes of this year. If anyone doubted that she could bounce back, she answered them in the only way she really knew: in her performances.

She approached training with even greater determination and desire to do it alone. She was still not cooperating with her coach and although they went through the motions together, in practice Debbie felt that their coach–athlete relationship was a sham. The only way to remain focused on her goals and aspirations was to pretend Coach Elliott did not exist. If she started to think about some of the things he said to her, her concentration wavered and her sprinting suffered.

In this way, 1998 proved to be her most successful collegiate season. At the NCAA Indoor Track and Field Championships, Debbie seized second in both the 55 and the 200 metres, and scored 16 of Georgia's 21 points to help give the Lady Bulldogs an eighth-place finish. In the SEC Outdoor Championships, she won both the 100 and the 200 metres, as well as finishing third as a member of the 4×400-metre relay team, and fifth as part of the 4×100 team. Her 22.5 points helped Georgia finish in third place in the SECs.

During the NCAA Outdoor Championships, Debbie achieved one of the most incredible performances in the history of Georgia track and field. At University Stadium in Buffalo, NY, Debbie became the first female track athlete to win national championships in the 100 and 200 metres since her idol Gwen Torrence in 1987, also for Georgia. She ran a wind-aided time of 10.94 to win the 100 metres, and Debbie's reaction was, 'Wow! That's awesome. Wind-aided or not, that's amazing!' and a time of 22.66 to win the 200 metres.

She remembers both races vividly and recalls that both victories were quite comfortable. She did not feel that anyone was near to her. Now, looking back, she can actually see something positive in her enforced rest the previous season. She believes that her body was actually telling her to slow down after all the years of non-stop training and competition. It did her limbs good to take the rest, and the results in 1998 would testify to that.

At the same outdoor championships in Buffalo, she was also part of the 4×100-metre relay team that finished fifth. In total, Debbie scored 21 of Georgia's 32 points to help them finish in a creditable sixth place overall.

Coming into the 1999 season, Debbie had already received a Georgia track and field record 15 All-American honours and won three national titles. Her training was going less smoothly: she was having some problems with her start. For some reason, she was not 'firing' properly and she could not get into her stride quickly enough. This has been an ongoing problem to this day and she readily admits that the start is the one area of her sprinting that gives her the most trouble.

Even now she would not go to Elliott: it was impossible for her to work happily with him at this time. Debbie felt that Norbert Elliott was her official coach in name only. Most of her workouts she devised herself. She had no one to observe and comment on the positives and negatives of her start or her form.

She is extremely grateful for the instruction she received from her first coach, Pancho Rahming. It was his words she remembered and tried to put into practice. Fortunately, in her final season at Georgia she managed to straighten out the start in time for the big meets, and saved her best performances for last.

She started off the 1999 campaign by equalling another Georgia track and field record, again held by Gwen Torrence, and claimed her fourth career national title with a championship in the indoor 60 metres. Four national titles also equalled a school record.

Perhaps the most fitting finale was at the 1999 SEC Outdoor Track and Field Championships, which, coincidentally, were held locally in Athens that year. Debbie was excited at the prospect of running on her home track in what she, and others, considered the most competitive of all the conference championships.

Her mother had come from The Bahamas for her graduation, which would take place a week later. Debbie treated her to a real pre-graduation bonus with one of her greatest weekends as a collegiate competitor. It was the finale she wanted: she won SEC Championships in both the 100 and 200 metres.

Coming into the championships, she had not felt very confident, especially in the 200 metres. Her confidence was not improved when the Jamaican Peta-Gaye Dowdie, from Louisiana State University, ran 22.43 seconds in the semi-final. Debbie was stunned at such a fast time. It was troubling because her own winning time in the NCAA Championships the previous year was only 22.53. She drew on all her reserves of determination and speed in the 200 metres final. She also let the home crowd inspire her, and the sentimental idea of this being her last appearance on her home track gave her even more determination than usual.

Finally, she drew inspiration from her mother's presence at a collegiate meet outside The Bahamas for the first time. All these factors inspired her competitive spirit for one last colossal effort. She went out and ran as only she knows how and set a conference record in the 100 metres. Then, in a run that she still cannot quite believe, she broke Gwen Torrence's 200-metre record with a time of 22.35, to claim the 200 title.

Throughout her time at Georgia, Debbie had wanted Torrence's records. The 100-metre record came easily in her first year. The 200 had seemed destined to elude her, but she took it in the end, in yet another example of the intense determination to achieve the goals she sets for herself. In addition to the individual races, Debbie also seized second as part of the 4×100-metre relay team, and third as part of the 4×400 team. Both relay times were new school records, and Debbie's 23.5 points meant that she won the SEC Commissioners Cup, awarded to the athlete with the most individual points at the SEC Championships.

Before her final collegiate meet, Debbie received the Jackie Joyner-Kersee Award for 1999 as the best women's track athlete in the nation. The NCAA flew her to San Diego to receive the Top VIII Award with the winners from seven other sports. The award recognises the top eight athletes in the NCAA, taking into account academic and athletic, as well as leadership achievements. To complete this accolade, Debbie was selected from among the eight to make the speech of acceptance on behalf of them all.

The final meet of her collegiate career, the NCAA Championships, was held in Boise, Idaho. Debbie went as the favourite for both the 100 and the 200 metres. When she talks about these final championships of her student life, she cannot hide the tinges of disappointment that she still feels. Despite running well, she could only claim two second places in the 100 and 200 metres, not the finishes she had hoped for or anticipated. She overcame the problems with her start, but she did not feel the real explosiveness that had been there for the SECs, and she was not completely happy with her performances.

She was also under pressure from her awareness of the scouts and agents from the European tour who would be watching. She knew that if she wanted to be invited to compete in Europe when she graduated, she would need to win. She need not have worried, because the invitations to go to Europe were made anyway, but she would have preferred the invitations to have been addressed to the NCAA champion and not the runner-up. A fourth-place finish as part of the 4×100-metre relay team completed her work at the NCAA finals. When the results were tabulated, Debbie accounted for 19.5 of Georgia's 37 points, to help lead them to a fourth-place team finish.

In her career at Georgia, Debbie gained an overall total of 121.5 points in NCAA competition. Previous to her collegiate career, Georgia's women's teams had never had a finish in the top 10 of the NCAAs. During her four-year career there, Georgia finished in the top six places in three out of the four years in the NCAA Outdoor Championships.

Furthermore, Debbie rewrote the Georgia track and field record books during her time as a Lady Bulldog. She currently holds, or is part of, five Georgia track and field records. She holds the record in the indoor 60 metres at 7.24 seconds, the 100 metres at 10.97 seconds, the 200 metres at 22.19 seconds, the 4×100-metre relay at 43.86 seconds, and the 4×400 at 3 minutes 33.83 seconds.

Her record in 1999, together with her graduation with honours and her numerous involvements in the field of community service, made her an ideal and obvious choice for the Joyner-Kersee Award. Just looking at this list of achievements emphasises the fact that

Debbie seized her chance, using and developing her talent to the fullest extent. University changed her life once again and, in spite of some negative aspects, set her on the path to fame and distinction that she has never regretted taking.

CHAPTER 5
OLYMPIC GAMES

Debut: Atlanta 1996

The Olympic Games embody the ultimate sporting test and experience. To represent his or her country at the Olympics is the dream and ambition of every athlete. The World Championships may occur more regularly, more money can be won at events like the Bislett Games in Oslo on the European circuit, but the Olympics, with their full exposure in the media, their history and reputation, and the promise of a medal to lock the athlete into immortality, provide the pinnacle of an athlete's ambition.

This chapter focuses on Debbie's experiences at the first three Olympics in which she competed: Atlanta in 1996, Sydney in 2000 and Athens in 2004. There were, of course, other prestigious meets in-between, such as the World Championships in Seville in 1999. These form part of Debbie's early life as a professional athlete and are related in the next chapter.

In 1996, the Olympics were held in Atlanta, Georgia, just a short drive along Route 8 from Athens and the University of Georgia. Debbie had qualified and, at 20, had already established herself as one of the premier female sprinters in The Bahamas. She was excited for a number of reasons. She had made the Olympics at her first attempt; the games were being staged in her 'neck of the woods', and her mother would be able to make the relatively short journey from Nassau to Atlanta.

She was elated to have made the team and was determined, as in all things, to go out and compete and do her very best. She felt confident in her ability to run at this level – after all, she had achieved the qualifying time – but she had not yet developed the self-confidence to feel that she really belonged in this company of athletes. She felt overawed by the pressure of occupying the same track as people she had grown up admiring and wishing to emulate: Merlene Ottey, Gail Devers and Gwen Torrence – older, more mature runners, with years of experience and all medal winners at previous Olympics.

So what did Debbie expect of herself as she lined up for her first heat in the 100 metres? She had an aim, which was to make it through the first round. But did she have a plan to ensure progress to the next round without taking too much out of herself? Did she actually believe she could win through to the next round? In fact, she was so nervous that all she was thinking about was reaching the finish line without stumbling, committing a false start or remaining fixed in the starting blocks, unable to move.

'I wasn't really thinking straight before that first heat. I was scared, excited, almost kind of drunk on the atmosphere,' she remembers. 'I certainly wasn't thinking of a race plan because my mind was too cluttered. I tried to do what Linford Christie says to do in his book: focus, get in the zone and see the finish. But I couldn't get my thoughts together. This was the Olympics and, almost unbelievably, I was on the track!'

Her nerves were understandable, of course, but she need not have worried. Supported by her instincts, she glided along the Atlanta track, seemingly carefree and confident of reaching round two. She crossed the line in third place. She had reached her first goal and she confesses that at that time it felt almost like making it to the final. Debbie quickly realised, however, that it was essential that she maintained her concentration and focused on the next race if she was to progress to the semi-final. The competition would now be much tougher.

She managed to concentrate more intensely in round two and again ran an outstanding race, finishing in the first four and securing her place in the semi-final. But words do not begin to describe the performance, because to Debbie it was a major accomplishment, one that she still describes as a dream come true, that was achieved as if climbing a ladder, one rung at a time. 'My first Olympics and I was in the last 16. One of the top 16 female sprinters in the world. It felt fantastic.'

Her excitement at this time was understandable: she had now 'arrived', and the Olympic final was realistically within reach. Unfortunately, the competition proved too strong in the semi-final and Debbie's seventh place was not enough to allow her to move on. But she had exceeded her wildest dreams. She had placed herself in the top 16 female sprinters in the world, a position she would steadily improve over the years and one of which she understandably remains very proud. She was happy and satisfied with what she had achieved.

Although her track career was still very much in its infancy, and she felt like a very immature racer, she knew that next time she would draw on this experience to deal with the pressures with more composure. She left the individual 100-metre arena with a clear goal for the next games in Sydney: to reach the final.

The real story of Debbie's first Olympics, and her second in Sydney, revolves around the 4×100-metre relay. There were five women in The Bahamas team in Atlanta, all capable of performing on the world stage: Debbie; Chandra Sturrup, who had come fourth in the 100-metre final and seventh in the 200; Savatheda Fynes; Eldece Clarke; and the matriarch of Bahamian women's athletics,

Pauline Davis. Pauline had established herself as one of the world's foremost female sprinters. She had been performing in the highest company for a number of years.

When Debbie ran the third leg in the semi-final and helped the team to qualify easily for the final, few could have predicted the controversy that was to follow before the final the next day. Certainly Debbie was taken by surprise.

She was sure of her place on the team: at the Bahamas National Championships, recognised by everyone as trials for the Olympic teams, she had come second in the 100 metres and had proved herself as the next fastest after Chandra Sturrup. Her reasoning was simple: if you were one of the four fastest, you were on the team. Others, however, had different approaches and different agendas. Although the coaches selected Debbie to run in the final, the other team members gave the coaches an ultimatum: if Debbie ran in the final, they would not.

To this day, Debbie is not sure of the reasoning behind this; nor has she been able to understand fully what she saw as betrayal by the other members of the team. She believed that the team should have abided by the decision of the coaches, but athlete power overturned their decision. Debbie was sidelined for the final. Eldece Clarke ran in her place.

Eldece and Pauline were old schoolmates from their time at the Government High School in Nassau. They were also the oldest members of the team. Could the ultimatum have had something to do with allegiance from school? Were they each so desperate for an Olympic medal that they would turn against the 'upstart new girl' and deny her a place in the final?

There were also some wildly far-fetched claims made about each runner's time in the semi-final. One was that Debbie's time for her 100 metres leg in the semi-final was the slowest of all the splits

– but she had had the advantage, a flying start over Eldece, the lead-off runner, whom she had beaten comfortably in the trials in any case.

Brent Stubbs, the sports editor of *The Tribune* newspaper in Nassau, remembers the scene on the practice track when the decision was made: 'There were all kinds of people on the practice track – athletes, coaches, managers – but she didn't wait until she got into the changing rooms to show her disappointment. She was heartbroken and she cried openly out there on the track. She wasn't going to hide it because she felt so strongly that she should have been in the team. But it made her stronger. Some other athletes might have given in, maybe even given up, but not Debbie. She somehow found the resolve to bounce back and she gained the respect of everyone in the track and field world by the way she did it. I spoke to her on that same evening when she had calmed down a little and she was quite philosophical about the decision. She told me, "Maybe it's just not my time."'

Debbie was running well in Atlanta. She had made the semi-finals of the individual 100 metres. She was the second fastest of the Bahamian sprinters. There was absolutely no reason for her not to be on the team. So Debbie, heartbroken to be missing out on a final in her first Olympics, fighting back tears of disappointment as another runner took the place that she felt she had rightfully earned, was relegated to watching the final from the stands. She had done everything right: she was running the times and yet she was not going to run in the biggest race of her life so far.

Of course, she cheered on the team as they passed the baton around the Atlanta track. Of course, she was delighted when Pauline crossed the finish line a mere 0.19 seconds behind the Americans to claim the silver. Of course, she was proud to receive a silver medal herself by virtue of the fact that she had run a leg in the semi-final, but the celebrations and congratulations had a hollow ring. For her, the medal was tarnished: not running in the final, not being on the podium with the other girls to be presented with the medal left her feeling empty, unfulfilled, cheated.

Nevertheless, it also left her feeling even more determined. Debbie herself says that the experience changed her whole outlook on running and made her resolve never to let anything like that happen to her again. She still feels that she should have been in that final relay team, but she made a pledge to herself: she would be a member of the relay team as long as she was still competing. Whatever it took – times, performances, sheer strength of personality – they were not going to repeat what they did to her in 1996.

Looking back on this episode, Debbie still finds it hard to hide the emotion, such was the disappointment. She has not forgotten what happened, but she has learned to forgive her teammates. As a team they were still quite immature. There were issues among them that would have to be resolved before the team would fulfil its enormous potential: the choice of the best four runners to comprise the team, the order in which they should run, the extent of team influence over the coaches. These are just some of the controversial and personal issues that managed to cause strife among the relay team.

In spite of her more than satisfactory individual performance, therefore, Debbie's first Olympics ended on a sour note of discontent. A positive outcome, however, was that the experience made Debbie a stronger athlete, competitor and person.

Afterwards, The Bahamas Amateur Athletic Association attempted to hold an investigation about what really happened and why Debbie qualified but was excluded at the last minute. Alpheus Finlayson, then president of the Bahamas Association of

Athletic Associations (BAAA), said, 'Letters were sent to all the women on the relay team, asking the women who threatened to refuse to run if Debbie was on the team to reply to tell us they had received the letters, and to describe to us what went on at the final practice before the relay final. But we got nowhere, because they all stuck together and didn't supply us with any new information. One of the women never even acknowledged her letter, claiming she never received it. However, the BAAA threatened to ban one of these women from The Bahamas team in future meets for a year, as it was clear from what we did know that she was the ringleader. It remained a threat, though, and we never banned her, although she took out an injunction against the BAAA, suing us for trying to prevent her from earning money. It could have become quite nasty, but, in the end, it died a natural death, was put away and forgotten and we all moved on.'

Sydney 2000

Debbie had been running very well in the lead-up to her second Olympic Games in Sydney, Australia. She felt prepared both physically and mentally. She firmly believed that these were to be her breakthrough games; this was to be her turn to claim an individual medal.

The games began, however, on a note of tragedy. Just two days before the first heats of the 100 metres, she received the news that her grandmother, who had had such a strong influence on her as a small child and for whom Debbie had retained such love, affection and respect, had passed away in her native Jamaica.

Debbie, naturally tearful, helpless and cut off from her family in Jamaica, had to pass the news on to her mother, who had arrived in Sydney to watch her. It was unthinkable for her not to attend her mother's funeral: she had only enough time to snatch a night's sleep and then catch a plane back across the world.

Debbie could not go with her, but was now in the position of having to miss a second grandparent's funeral. It was also understandably upsetting that her mother would now be unable to watch her events live. Debbie hoped that amidst all the preparations for the funeral in Westmoreland, her mother would be able to watch the races on television.

Deeply shocked and saddened, she spent a tearful couple of days trying to focus on preparing for the most important races of her life. She often found herself thinking, however, of the days in the Westmoreland fields, collecting chickens' eggs with the grandmother who had meant so much to her as a child, and who would now find her final resting place in those same fields, alongside her husband.

In the four years since Atlanta, the 200 metres had become Debbie's stronger event. During the European season before the Games she had beaten all her competitors, except Marion Jones, in the longer sprint. Her involvement in the 100 metres as well meant double the load, but she believed in herself and knew that, in spite of the shock and sadness she felt at her grandmother's passing, she was capable of doing well.

Debbie has mixed feelings about her individual performances in Sydney. She is very proud that she made the finals of both sprints, and still takes solace from the fact that not many female sprinters can make such a boast. She had made progress from the previous Olympics. Nevertheless, there is a feeling of intense disappointment that she did not fulfil her expectations and win a medal, or do a little better in at least one of the distances.

135

Despite feeling tense and a little under-prepared, her path to the finals had been straightforward. In the 100 metres she joined teammates Chandra and Savatheda to make a Bahamian trio vying for the medals. That three young Bahamian women were among the eight finalists of an Olympic event was a significant achievement for Bahamian track and field. The Bahamas, with a population of about 150,000 females, thus made up 38 per cent of the field for the race, an extraordinarily high percentage for such a small country. The trio themselves were elated to be together for such a momentous occasion.

Marion Jones was the only US athlete in the final. What happened in that final is, of course, well known. Marion Jones ran an incredible race and won by 37-hundredths of a second, a very wide margin for such a short race. The Bahamians ran in 6th, 7th and 8th. Debbie brought up the rear and, while she was proud to have made her first Olympic final, she was very disappointed with her time.

They knew that Bahamians back in Nassau, Freeport and the Family of Islands would be disappointed with the result: people had been expecting at least one medal, after all. They were all disappointed not to have delivered, but they were shocked and upset when they saw the headline in *The Nassau Guardian* the next day. In two-inch high capitals, it read: 'Black Sunday'. The report emphasised, unreasonably and unfairly, the failure of the women to gain medals, ignoring the achievement of their reaching the final and placing themselves among the eight fastest female sprinters in the world.

'The gods certainly weren't smiling on The Bahamas on Saturday night at the Olympic Stadium … Chandra Sturrup, Savatheda Fynes and Debbie Ferguson finished at the bottom of the field', the report continued. With its negative focus on details such as all three athletes' slow reaction time to the starting gun, and emphasising the margin of Marion Jones's victory, the report paid only cursory attention to the significance of all three of them making the final in the first place. When they had recovered from the shock, the three women were understandably angry and felt let down by the unappreciative reporters from their own country.

There was, however, little time to dwell on the outcome of the 100 metres, because Debbie immediately found herself racing in the heats for the 200. This was her better event and, even though it is a tougher race, her strength and stamina allowed her to make the most of the bend and the long home straight.

Progress to the final was quite straightforward, or so it seemed to those watching in the early hours via satellite on Cable Bahamas. Although she never showed it, Debbie was struggling after the four races in the 100 that she had already completed, and still coping with the emotional upset brought about by her grandmother's death.

For the first time in her career, she found herself struggling between heats to recover her energy and replenish the spring and power in her legs. Nevertheless, she claimed her rightful place in the final alongside fellow Bahamian Pauline Davis, who was making her final appearance in individual Olympic competition. Although Debbie's time in the semi-final was not one of the three fastest, her record during the build-up to the games, and her reputation, made her a favourite to win a medal. The night before the final, however, she was in tears again, overwhelmed by sadness at her grandmother's death. She called Mrs Bethel in Nassau and told her how she was feeling. 'I told her I couldn't focus on the race because I kept thinking about my grandmother and the funeral I had missed.'

As always, Mrs Bethel offered comfort and calm advice, but ended by telling Debbie to go out there the next day and run for her grandmother, and bring home a medal for her. It was the sort of message that Debbie needed and it served to focus her thoughts on the final. So what went wrong on that balmy Australian night? Debbie makes no excuses: it had nothing to do with emotional stress or tired legs. She just ran a bad race.

Why did this happen? Was it the weight of expectation? Was it the presence of her teammate and mentor a couple of lanes to her left? Did she have a bad start? Debbie explains it like this: 'I felt like I gave away that race. I feel that I should have placed top three. I was just so surprised at the speed at which Marion Jones came out and how early in the race she moved past me that I lost concentration and focus for long enough to slip out of my rhythm. By the time I snapped back, it was too late. I had lost too much ground. Not that this is an excuse – it's what happened and I paid for it mightily by finishing a disappointing fifth.'

Debbie's personal disappointment was more than compensated for by Pauline Davis's second place. Bahamians were able to delight in the country's first ever Olympic track medal, won by their inspirational female leader who made her final 200 metres the race of her life. Debbie was the first to congratulate her. Fighting back her own disappointment, she embraced her teammate warmly and sincerely. Her face showed the smiles of joy for Pauline's achievement, but inside she felt spent, empty, devastated.

There was still a third chance for a medal, but the question on everyone's mind was whether she would recover in time to take that chance in the 4×100-metre relay. Fortunately, Eldece Clarke was there in Sydney and could run in the heats so that Debbie could rest after the gruelling 200 metres. She needed all the time she could in order to recover both mentally and physically. In spite of her training and dedication, she was at a low ebb.

As she prepared with her teammates and felt her strength returning, she knew they had a great opportunity to win gold. They were already the World Champions and three of the team had made it to the final of the 100 metres. They believed in themselves and had grown much closer as a unit since Atlanta. They had begun to get along much better with each other and there was far less stress in the group. There were still one or two issues, however, and Debbie remembers controversy again rearing its unattractive head just before the final.

Even though Eldece had run the two rounds in Debbie's place – which the team had won easily – there was never any question of Debbie not running in the final. She had fulfilled the pledge she made to herself after Atlanta, and as she had been in Seville in the World Championships a year earlier, she was a fixture in the team as the runner to take the baton to the tape – the anchor.

Nevertheless, Pauline wanted to change the winning formula, switch Debbie to the third leg and run the final leg herself. Debbie can understand Pauline's desire. She had run a brilliant 200 metres in the individual final and claimed the silver. She had anchored the team in the two heats on the way to the final. It was her last race in her Bahamas uniform. What better way to commemorate it than by capturing the headlines and the photo space in the papers, breaking the tape as the gold medal champions?

History has a strange way of repeating itself, but it also has an even stranger way of altering events just slightly, even ironically. This time, when Pauline made her suggestion, Savatheda and Chandra would hear nothing of it, saying that the coach had assigned her a leg to run and that was the leg she should run.

Speaking with her usual candour, Debbie confesses that she would not have minded Pauline running that final leg because she is always acutely aware of the pressure that the last leg places on an athlete. 'If anything goes wrong, it's the last runner who is remembered. If the last runner gets run down, then she takes the blame for losing the team the gold medal.'

However, the coaches stood by the other members and declared that if the team was not going to run in the selected order, it would not run at all. Once that announcement was made there was no more dissension. One of the team sponsors, the successful businessman and Bahamas resident Peter Nygard, took the team out to dinner. The purpose was to provide an opportunity for the team to talk about their differences and then put them aside, forget about what had happened in the past and pull together as a team that could focus on the most important task: winning the gold.

It must have been successful: the next day, the four Bahamians ran the race of their lives to bring the gold to The Bahamas. All four were completely focused and energised, encouraging each other as they mentally rehearsed their changeovers and walked on to the track to make their final preparations. Debbie was nervous, the adrenaline was pumping, but she remained focused. She anticipated the most important race of her life with enthusiasm and, above all, confidence.

Suddenly, it seemed, it was Saturday morning in Nassau, and the whole population of the archipelago turned on their televisions for the women's 4×100-metre relay final. The Bahamian team faced stiff competition, not only from the US, but also from China, the Russian Federation, France and long-standing rivals Jamaica. Abaco's Savatheda Fynes was the lead-off runner. By the time she handed over to Chandra Sturrup, she had made up the stagger on the US team. Debbie could not see Savatheda from her position at the final changeover point, but on the huge monitor above the track she could see that Fynes had given the team a great start.

It had been widely speculated that the Bahamians would need a 5-metre lead at the last exchange to be sure of victory. Savatheda had given them just that.

Debbie, her excitement mounting, could hardly tear her eyes away from the screen as Chandra ran the perfect straight, maintaining the lead, but she realised just in time that she must watch the track and prepare herself completely for her leg. She did not want to get caught with the runners right behind her and her attention still on the screen!

Tense, with her nerves beginning to gnaw in her stomach, she realised that she had bitten off two of her nails while watching Chandra as she handed on to curve-running specialist, Pauline. She waited for what seemed like an eternity as Pauline approached the changeover box. As the runners came off the curve for the final exchange, it was clear that Jamaica had made up ground. The US team was out of contention, at least 5 metres back, but the race was far from over. Debbie thought to herself, 'Everything has got to be perfect. We're in the lead, but we can easily lose it if the changeover is not perfect. Now, don't let yourself down. Don't let your country down. Take the baton and just run!'

She watched Pauline's feet reach the mark. She set off just as she had all those times in practice, timing it so that she would be at top speed when Pauline placed the stick in her hand. Underneath all the thoughts of technical perfection were other thoughts. She had only managed last place in the 100-metre final; would she be quick enough to hold off the other runners now? She remembered painfully how Marion Jones had blown everyone away in the 200-metre final. Would the 5-metre lead be enough?

The pressure was on her, but as the roars and screams from the crowd increased and Pauline and Debbie became one, linked by the metal tube, silence filled Debbie's ears. Even though many experts and track reporters described it as a somewhat 'deliberate' exchange, Debbie was immediately in stride, with a 2-metre lead over Merlene Ottey of Jamaica.

Incredibly, Debbie remained in her cone of silence all along the home stretch, hearing none of the roars as the eight runners pounded along the tartan. Debbie has often watched recordings of the race. She can see the crowd cheering and hear the noise, but in her mind was silence and she could have heard a pin drop.

She remained in her zone of silence all the way to the finish, maintaining the 2-metre lead to the line. Looking back, she regards it as the best 100 metres she has ever run, a mixture of fear and excitement producing the performance of a lifetime. She went out and just ran, ran her heart out and completed the job her teammates had begun just half a minute before she received the baton.

Her respected opponent, Merlene Ottey, held on for second, with Marion Jones closing fast to give the US team the bronze. The winning time was 41.95 seconds, the fastest in the world in 2000.

Sometimes, when Debbie watches the tape of that race, she does not actually recognise herself as the runner coming in first. It seems that her intense focus and place in that zone have somehow transformed her, given her a special power, physique and ability that all came together on that night.

Pictures of the finish show Debbie rejoicing, arms wide and face aglow with the excitement, but actually the magnitude of the achievement had not then struck her. Approaching the finish line, she knew no one had passed her on either side. She knew The Bahamas was first, but it took a while to register what that meant. She even remembers at the moment of victory wondering if she should throw up her arms in salute. 'I slowly grasped the fact that we had won,' she says. '"Oh my God," I thought, "we won, we won!"'

And as she slowed down and turned back to find her teammates, she squealed in delight, 'We won! We won the Olympics!' Chandra, Savatheda and Pauline arrived and the four of them embraced, laughed, cried and rejoiced, as they realised the enormity of what they had accomplished. This was every athlete's dream and, even though it was not an individual gold, it was a gold medal, and The Bahamas' first ever on the track.

Wrapped in Bahamian flags, they set off on their lap of honour, so excited that they did not feel the track beneath their feet. They were so exhilarated by their performance, they kept reminding each other, 'We won! We won the Olympic gold medal!' They were in a different world, intoxicated by the sound of the crowd, the replay of the race on the huge screen and their own infectious delight.

Even the normally reserved and undemonstrative Chandra and Savatheda were shrieking with delight. They held hands, embraced each other, and hugged friends and teammate Eldece Clarke in the crowd. Debbie describes her emotions as 'the best feeling in the world', a sentiment that is certainly reflected in her smile, her body language and her muscle-flexing poses for the cameras.

Anyone who has participated in sporting activities or in competitions of even a semi-serious nature enjoys the thrill of winning the final game, the final race, the championship match. Collecting a cup, plaque or medal with friends and family there to cheer and enjoy the moment is a special feeling, no matter where it occurs – the parking lot after a road race, the basketball court after the final game, or the track and field stadium after a school meet.

It does not matter how many, or how few, people are there to witness the event. When Debbie and her relay partners walked across the Sydney track and Richard 'Dick' Pound, now the vice-president of the International Olympic Committee, presented them with their gold medals, 110,000 people were packed into the largest stadium ever built to host an Olympic Games. The eyes of the world were on them via satellite on TV screens in every continent. Pound was accompanied by Bahamian Alpheus Finlayson, president of The Bahamas Amateur Athletic Association, who presented the team with their bouquets. It was Debbie's proudest moment on stage in her life.

She was, of course, sad to reflect that her grandmother had not been alive to see the race, and that her mother had had to return to the Caribbean for the funeral. But the little girl from 'Over-the-Hill', Nassau, had won the highest prize in track and field. Not even that sadness could quench her pride and satisfaction as she stood on the podium with her teammates. The disappointments of the individual sprints evaporated with every touch of the coveted gold medal. The Golden Girls, as they had been dubbed in The Bahamas, with Debbie at the helm once more, had confirmed their place at the top of the sprinting world.

As The Golden Girls left Sydney, they were already looking ahead to Athens 2004, the birthplace of the Olympic Games, just four years away. Debbie was already planning her strategies for another three-way assault on the sprints, but no one could foresee what would happen in the intervening four years: Pauline Davis retired, Eldece Clarke retired, Savatheda Fynes and Chandra Sturrup were plagued by injuries that disrupted their training and affected their performances. Savatheda was not fit enough even to qualify for Athens. Chandra was a shadow of her former self, unable to run in the individual events. After a highly successful year in 2002, Debbie herself went through a terrible season in 2003. After the successes of Sydney 2000, things did not look too promising for the relay team in Athens 2004.

The home of the Olympics: Athens 2004

Greece and Athens have special places in the hearts of all track and field athletes: it was in Greece that the Olympics came into being, even before the written records that began in 776 BC.

The first Olympic champion in history was Coroebus, who won the only event at the first recorded Olympics, the stade. This was a run of approximately 192 metres (210 yards). These ancient games, with their religious origin, continued to be contested for nearly 1,200 years until AD 393. By then, a number of other events and sports had been included, but they were abolished by the Roman Emperor Theodosius I, who considered them to be pagan and offensive to his Christian beliefs.

It was not until about 1,500 years later that a young Frenchman, Pierre de Coubertin, became the leading activist in the reintroduction of what were to be called the Modern Olympic Games. The site chosen for their rebirth was obviously their original home, Athens, Greece.

The first Olympic Games of the modern era opened in the first week of April 1896. Since the Greek government had been unable to fund construction of a stadium, a wealthy Greek architect, Georgios Averoff, donated funds to restore the Panathenaic Stadium, originally built in 330 BC, with white marble.

As the Games were not well publicised internationally, contestants were not nationally chosen, but came individually and at their own expense. Some contestants were even tourists who happened to be in the area during the Games. Athletes wore the uniform of their athletic club rather than any national strip.

All this, of course, is very different from the games as we know them today. In 1896, 241 athletes from 14 nations competed. In

2004, over 10,500 athletes from nearly 200 countries competed for 17 days. In 1896, there were 45 separate events. In 2004, there were over 300. The cost of staging the 2012 games in London was the equivalent of US $14 billion.

With the opportunity to mingle with fellow competitors in the Olympic Village and enjoy the unique atmosphere that such a large number of dedicated and talented athletes bring to the setting, it is no wonder that Debbie absolutely thrives on the atmosphere of the Olympic Games. She regards Atlanta, Sydney and Athens as the pinnacles of her career.

The spirit of competition is in itself inspiring. The Olympic Oath could almost have been written for her: 'In the name of all competitors, I promise that we shall take part in these Olympic Games, respecting and abiding by the rules that govern them, in the true spirit of sportsmanship, for the glory of sport and the honour of our teams.'

In addition to the oath, there is the Olympic Creed, which states, 'The most important thing in the Olympic Games is not to win but to take part, just as the most important thing in life is not the triumph but the struggle. The essential thing is not to have conquered but to have fought well.' This obviously has a special meaning for someone like Debbie, who has struggled to achieve their goals.

Athens 2004 will always have a special place in Debbie's heart. The memories began at the opening ceremony of the games: the honour of carrying the Bahamian flag had been conferred on her. To many, this honour surpasses any other distinction, including even winning medals. The flag-bearer is not necessarily the best athlete, but someone who displays longevity or who has overcome severe obstacles in order to compete at a high level. This was the first time Debbie had actually been present for the opening ceremony, but she genuinely had not even considered herself as a possible candidate, thinking that maybe Chandra Sturrup would have been asked as she was the oldest on the team, or maybe Mark Knowles, the tennis player, who had won the Australian Open Men's Doubles title. But the honour was given to Debbie, in recognition of her commitment, reliability and success in Bahamian colours over the previous eight years.

She took the banner and held it up proudly, just as she had taken up opportunities that had come her way since first winning the scholarship to St Andrew's back in 1988. Carrying the Bahamian flag at such a public occasion seemed to cement her feelings about nationality: the slight ambivalence she used to feel and the affinity to her Jamaican roots disappeared in that lap of patriotic fervour under the aquamarine, black and gold, at the head of her nation's athletes.

During the parade, Debbie cast her mind back to Sydney, remembering that Pauline Davis had carried the Bahamian flag. Debbie reminded herself that Pauline had gone on to win silver in the 200 metres. Ever ready to respond to positive signs, Debbie believed from that moment that she would win an individual medal in Athens. She did not tell anyone, but she genuinely believed it would come to pass. The wonderful beginning to the games served as a positive prelude to the hard work of competition, which provided once again the highs and lows of results. Debbie had arrived in Athens feeling better about her chances in the 100 metres: she had enjoyed a successful European season on the Grand Prix circuit at that distance. As for the 200, she had not run many and felt that there were too many women running faster times that summer.

As in all her international competitions, however, her competitive spirit, genuine sprinting ability and tremendous pride

147

in herself to maintain her standards and level of performance saw her through all the rounds to the finals in both sprints. She showed the world once more, just as she had in Sydney, that at both distances she was in the elite class of the top eight female sprinters in the world.

Nevertheless, Debbie's status in the world of women's sprinting had changed since Atlanta and Sydney. In the Athens finals, now a relatively old 28, she was very much the elder stateswoman. After watching the final of the 100 metres on television, Chandra Sturrup and Laverne Eve (another of Debbie's Bahamian teammates) told her that the commentator had informed the world that Debbie Ferguson was 'the oldest competitor in the race'. In eight short years, she had gone from feeling, in her own words, 'very much the new kid on the block in Atlanta', to the most experienced and mature athlete on the track.

After the 200 metres final, Chandra and Laverne informed Debbie that this time the commentator had told all the viewers that Debbie Ferguson was 'the only female sprinter from the finals of the 100 and 200 metres in Sydney to make both finals again in Athens.' Debbie has always been aware that a track career is short, but this fact really brought it home to her and made her proud of her consistently high level of performance over the years, but also made her very much aware of how quickly and suddenly things can change.

The finals themselves were both very competitive races. In the 100, Debbie ran for all she was worth, running her best time of the year and improved her finishing position in Sydney by one place. This time she finished seventh.

Although she was disappointed not to have won a medal or to have finished closer to achieving one, she did take solace from her improved position and her time. She also remembers superstitiously checking omens and realising that there were three Jamaican women in the final, just as there had been three Bahamians in the 100-metre final in Sydney. Although she said nothing to her teammates, she felt inside that the Jamaicans were going to follow in the Bahamians' footsteps and win the relay gold.

In the 200, she was drawn in the outside lane by virtue of her fourth place finish in the semi-final, but it is interesting to note that only the winner of the other semi-final had run faster than Debbie. The outside lane draw troubled her at first, however, and she started feeling sorry for herself. 'Why lane eight?' she asked herself. 'Even lane one would be better; at least I would be able to see the other runners.'

If she had continued too long with these thoughts, she might well have talked herself out of any chance of a medal, but eventually she managed to put all negative thoughts out of her mind by telling herself, 'You know what, I've come this far. Stop griping about the lane and not liking it. Now it's too late. I can't do anything about it. Just go out there and perform. I have experience. I know what I'm capable of doing. Stop focusing on your weakness such as your start, because every time you focus on that you make it seem bigger than it actually is and you don't do what you're supposed to do.'

Debbie had in fact decided that she did not want any advice, even from the coaches, before this 200-metre final. She wanted to run her own race and what the coaches were telling her was just confusing her. She did not want a race plan. She just wanted to go out and run as fast as she could for 22 seconds, without any instructions cluttering her mind. Strangely enough, while she was stripping away all conflicting and confusing instructions from her mind, there was one person to whom she did turn for advice: by now, her ex-fiancé, George, still back in Nassau.

Over the years, George has come to know very well how Debbie thinks. It seemed quite natural for her to contact him and ask his advice. Although no longer a couple, Debbie trusted him as a coach. She knew that if there was anything in her running that needed a little attention, George was the one who would spot it.

So she called George and told him that what she was doing just was not working. He talked about the start that had been worrying her. He gave her three small tips that she was able to practise before the race and which led her to get out of the blocks in one of the best starts of her career.

She blazed out with no one to draw on and kept the lead for about 100 metres, 'And then I started thinking,' she laments, 'and it's not good to think.' Debbie remembers those thoughts, which were along the lines of: 'Oh my God, they haven't caught me yet! Debbie, what are you doing? Don't think about it, run!'

She reckons that that split-second loss of concentration was probably enough to cost her the silver medal. She does not go so far as to say the gold, because Veronica Campbell was running so superbly. All things considered, this was a great run, a thrilling run, a special run, a run to remember. The oldest competitor in the race had shown them and had claimed her first individual Olympic medal. The sense of self-belief that she'd felt when carrying the flag at the opening ceremony had come true.

And so to the defence of the 4×100-metre relay crown: by this time, Debbie was ready to relax and admits that her goal in the relay was to have fun. She was entirely professional, as ever, but she approached the races in a light-hearted way, feeling no pressure, looking to enjoy the event. Debbie's own expectations for the team were not high. Pauline had retired, Savatheda was injured and not even at the games, and Chandra was some way short of her best. Only Debbie from The Golden Girls was running at peak performance, and her new teammates were not really fast enough yet to give the team more than an outside chance of snatching a medal. Strangely, Debbie felt less pressure than she had in Sydney.

The Bahamian coaches had enough confidence in their runners to rest Debbie from the first round after her exertions in the individual competitions. They feared, however, that the team would not qualify for the final if Debbie did not run. She therefore dragged her tired limbs into the semi-final to ensure the team's final place.

In spite of all this, she still maintains that it was less to do with her and more to do with the team – even though she was anchoring and was the only runner from the old team to be performing at their previous level. More importantly, though, the team was not expected to do well, even though the Bahamian media took a contrary view and wildly overrated the team's chances of winning a medal.

Debbie's anchor leg in the semi-final assured the team of their place in the final. A poor first leg, however, left the others with too much to do, despite a phenomenal effort down the home stretch from Debbie, who says, 'We still came very close to taking the bronze. We were just a split-second behind. If we'd had another few metres, I think we would have got third.'

Debbie won the admiration of all who watched the race for her superhuman efforts on the last leg, and, while there is a tinge of disappointment when she talks about it, she feels proud to have been a part of the team and what it actually achieved against the odds. As a postscript, it is worth noting that Debbie's premonition about the Jamaican girls proved correct: they won the gold with something to spare.

Looking back on the games, Debbie feels they were the happiest for the women sprinters. There was more of a genuine team feeling, and even though the medals eluded them, they were a closer, more tightly knit group.

'We didn't have any fuss or the quarrels that affected us in previous years,' says Debbie. 'Three of the team only had the relay to focus on and weren't distracted by individual events, so we were all able help and encourage each other. It was almost issue-free, except that there were five of us and only four can run at any one time.

'One of the girls, Philippa Arnette, was supposed to run in the semi-final. She was withdrawn by the coaches. I ran instead because they didn't think we would go through if I didn't run. Philippa was very upset. She went to the Olympics and didn't even run a leg. I sympathise with her, but there wasn't anything I could do.

'It just seems there's always going to be something to cause strife. But it happens to all teams. The Jamaicans had theirs when Beverly McDonald, their most experienced and best curve runner, didn't get to run in the final in Athens. The Jamaican coaches picked all the younger women and left her out. The Jamaicans, who, incidentally, ran the fastest time ever for a Jamaican relay team, were fussing amongst themselves right up to the final.

'The Americans too, were arguing about whether Marion Jones should run or not. [Marion Jones had not been selected for the individual sprints because of a poor showing in the US National Championships.] So these things are normal and we just have to live with the decisions that are made.'

Three Olympic Games and three medals: quite an achievement. So what was left to aim for? Debbie planned to continue running at least until 2008 and the Beijing Olympics. She felt that she could remain at the top for one more assault on an individual gold medal, but she was also aware of the risks of 'overstaying her welcome', and reluctant to tarnish a glittering career by performing below the level she had maintained over the years. She wanted to retire as an asset to her country and the track team, and continue working with determination and dedication to achieve that aim.

CHAPTER 6
THE PROFESSIONAL ATHLETE

A difficult decision

Debbie left the University of Georgia in the summer of 1999, after five years of record-breaking achievement. During the last few months before graduating, she had finally decided not to pursue her dream of going to medical school, but first to test the waters on the European track circuit and follow a different dream by becoming a professional athlete.

She had spent many hours deliberating, but at last felt comfortable with her decision. It had not been easy. There were expectations from significant people in her life that she would continue her studies and realise the original dream – to which they had all contributed.

First, her mother had supported and provided for her throughout her life. Second, Orinthia Nesbeth had been the source of the scholarship to St Andrew's, and of much other financial support. Third, Earla Bethel had inspired Debbie by example. All these people were anxious for her to move on to medical school and eventually become a paediatrician.

Taking the opposite view were people such as her boyfriend George, other athletes, her coaches and agents, and, most important of all, Debbie herself, who now recognised that the world was at her feet, fame was beckoning and riches were there for the taking.

The second group reckoned that the chance was too good to miss. She was still only 23, so there would be plenty of time to return to the original plan after a few seasons of running.

Debbie rationalises the situation in this way: 'I believed in my God-given talent. I thought about my grandmother's words when I was a small child and remembered how she had told me never to waste my talents. I genuinely believed that I could make a good living as a professional. I just couldn't pass up the opportunity to put it to the test. I knew I was going to disappoint some people and, believe me, that was the hardest part, but when those agents for the different athletic shoe companies started showing interest, I knew I was going to be a runner.'

Fortunately, by this time, she had stopped feeling guilty about the decision. 'I spoke to Mrs Nesbeth, my mom and Mrs Bethel, and told them how I was feeling. I explained that at last I understood that I was born to run and could not miss this chance. I could see they were upset, but they didn't say it. They voiced their support for me, in fact.'

In that summer of 1999, Debbie still believed that she had simply put her medical studies in the pending tray and would reopen the file a short time later. By 2005, she knew that she would not. Track became her life and her living. She no longer had the desire nor the stamina for a further long period of study at a medical school. The sponsors and mentors who wished so strongly that their special protégée would fulfil her dreams came to appreciate that these dreams had changed. Valuable as the career in medicine would be, they could see that she was already held in high esteem by Bahamians, through her commitment to her chosen discipline. The summer of 1999 provided the best opportunities to prove this commitment to everyone.

As soon as the season at Georgia was over, and with Debbie still feeling disappointment at finishing second in both the 100 and the 200 metres in the NCAA Championships, an agent from the Adidas shoe company came to call. He offered to be her equipment provider and produced a very inviting contract. Adidas and Nike perennially vie for the position of top equipment sponsor in the athletic world. Debbie was happy to affiliate herself with the former. Thus, it was in Adidas sprints that she went to the Pan American Games in Winnipeg a little later that summer. She had, of course, run in Winnipeg before – in 1993, in the Pan American Junior Championships, when she won bronze in the 200 metres. This time, she blazed out of the blocks in the final of the 200 metres and went two places better. In a time of 22.83 seconds, she won the gold medal and firmly set the tone for what was to be a golden summer.

'It was just the start I wanted,' says Debbie. 'I had run a couple of races in Europe and was feeling my way a little, but back on familiar territory in Winnipeg I felt very confident and very strong.

'It wasn't that I felt I had to prove myself immediately but I wanted to do well to help make my godparents [Mrs Nesbeth and Mrs Bethel] feel that I had made the right decision.'

Certainly, a gold medal did no damage to that desire. When the Winnipeg championships had finished, Debbie returned to Europe for more meets. Although she often felt like a new girl and admits to feeling overawed by her opponents and the occasions, she quickly started to relish the atmosphere and, of course, the travelling.

'I found myself waking up in Paris on Friday and then moving on to Rome by the following Wednesday,' enthuses Debbie. 'I realised very quickly that I was loving every minute of it. Track was giving me the chance to see the world. I tried hard to fit in some sightseeing. This wasn't easy, given our tight schedules, but I always tried to see some famous parts of the cities where I was staying.'

In 2001, Debbie eventually decided to move on from Coach Elliott. Back in the summer of 1999, he remained her coach. After returning to Europe, running in a few more meets and gradually finding her feet on the circuit, Debbie was an automatic choice for the Bahamian team at the World Championships in Seville. She was entered for the 100 and the 200 metres and was feeling in very good shape and form for the tests to come.

'I had run some impressive times for the 200, especially in Europe. I had a feeling that this was my time to tell the world I was there. I took it one race at a time, as usual, and won my way through to the semi-final of the 100 metres and to the final of the 200.

'In my semi-final, Marion Jones, who was the clear favourite, pulled up with a back problem and didn't finish, which left me thinking that maybe I was right, maybe this was my time.'

But the final was a different story. Even though Marion Jones was not in the line-up, another American, Inga Miller, tore along the track and won the gold. Debbie was embroiled in a blanket finish with three other runners, separated by just six-hundredths of a second. Debbie was eventually placed fifth.

'That was a big disappointment,' she laments. 'I felt I had a great chance, but I wasn't ready for Inga's strong showing. I actually beat her in a Grand Prix meet a couple of weeks after the Worlds, but in the race when it really mattered, I didn't do my best. But the important thing is not to let the disappointments become setbacks. I try to focus on the positive and take good things even from defeats. But this one hurt, especially with Marion out of the running, so it was disappointing to lose to her teammate.'

The race that all Bahamians were waiting for, however, and the race that Debbie remembers best, was the women's 4×100-metre relay. The Bahamian squad had settled itself into what was to become a very familiar line-up, and the five women were all on very good form. They also seemed to have settled some of the differences that marred their performance in Athens two years previously.

Debbie, as she had promised herself after the disappointment of Atlanta, had cemented herself into the team as the anchor runner. She tells how the order for the runners came about. 'My running the last leg gave us better options. We could benefit from Chandra's speed along the straight and Pauline's ability on the curve. Savatheda and I could run at either end, but Savatheda was always the better starter.'

Everyone agreed on this order and they all adhered to it. Debbie rested for the semi-final, having expended energy in seven races already. Eldece Clarke took her place, but Debbie was back in the team for the final. And what a final it was! Debbie recalls, 'Even without Marion Jones, the Americans were still the favourites, but everything clicked for us that night. We were too good for all the other teams. In fact, the US team came in fourth, with the French and the Jamaicans our closest rivals.

'I was very excited. We all were, because it was our first gold medal as a relay team and only the second gold won by The Bahamas in the World Championships. Troy Kemp won the first in 1995 in Gothenburg in the high jump, so this was a major achievement and we enjoyed the moments afterwards for all they were worth. We were all still a little naive and we weren't actually very sure how to celebrate. We were quite a bit more restrained than we were after the Olympic victory the next year.'

It was after this victory that they were dubbed The Golden Girls by the Bahamian press. Restrained or not, The Golden Girls were the World Champions and their achievement set the whole country talking. Fred Mitchell, now the Minister of Foreign Affairs in The

Bahamas government, but in 1999 simply an opposition spokesman, described it like this on his webpage, Fred Mitchell Uncensored:

> *It was the topic of every breakfast, lunchtime, school-time and work-time conversation. The country was in the thrall of victory. It was a rare moment of patriotic pride, as the country swelled its collective chest when the five young ladies brought home the gold, with Debbie Ferguson sprinting the final leg to victory.*

The Bahamas pulled out all the stops to celebrate the gold medal achievement, feting The Golden Girls with a victory parade and rally through the streets of New Providence, and placing large portraits at the Nassau International Airport, where visitors arriving in the country can still see them. Debbie revelled in the celebrations, as they capped a remarkable first season as a professional athlete. How she hoped they would all be like this first one!

The one aspect of the gold medal success that irked was the American relay team's claim that The Bahamas would not have won had Marion Jones been able to compete. The American sprinters taunted all Bahamians, not just the relay team: they would show the world who the real champions were at the Sydney Olympics the following year. 'All their talk just made us even more determined,' says Debbie. 'We knew we deserved the medal and we sure weren't going to let them talk us out of believing that. Beating them in Sydney when they had Marion Jones in their team was even sweeter after their mocking in Seville.'

A new coach

After the summer of 1999, Debbie's years would be divided into roughly equal thirds: January to May was serious training in the US in preparation for the track and field season. May to September was the competitive season, which Debbie would spend mainly in Europe, although she also travelled to championships in other parts of the world with the Bahamas team. September to the end of December would be spent at home in Nassau, recuperating from the exertions of the season and involving herself in the myriad activities that make up her life.

Debbie began her professional athletic career by retaining her training base in Georgia, amidst the familiar surroundings of the university. Norbert Elliott was still her coach, and despite all the problems inherent in their relationship, his actual training methods and the regimen he set for her were obviously proving successful.

In spite of this, Debbie eventually had to move on and chose the latter part of 2001, after her silver medal in the 200 metres in the World Championships in Edmonton, Canada, to announce a change of coach and a change of location for her winter preparations.

'Those World Championships marked my best performance as an individual on the world stage,' explains Debbie. 'It was a breakthrough time for me. I reached the final of the 100 metres and finished sixth, but most people remember the race because this was the race when Marion Jones was beaten. Pintusevich-Block from Ukraine beat her – she actually beat her in the semi-final and the final – so we all realised that Marion was not invincible. Chandra Sturrup, my relay buddy, also reached the final, but finished just outside the medals too, in fourth place.'

The build-up to the 200 metres was, naturally, full of media expectation, following Jones's unexpected defeat in the shorter sprint. Speculation regarding the possibility of another upset became even more intense following the semi-finals, when Debbie won her race in the fastest time, faster than Marion Jones's winning time in her semi.

Debbie remembers that it felt so easy and smooth. 'I couldn't believe I had won with what seemed so little difficulty,' she says, 'but that appears to be the way it is with me. When I run well, when all things are in synch, it is so effortless that I don't realise I'm running fast. It's a feeling I try to recapture all the time, but it doesn't occur very often.'

Brent Stubbs of Nassau's *Tribune* newspaper reflects: 'All of us in the press box were anticipating the final of the 200. The Bahamian contingent were sure Debbie was going to get the gold. I had a couple of bets with other writers, as we always do, but this time it wasn't bravado, I genuinely felt Debbie would do it.'

Debbie remembers the electric atmosphere on the track and the adrenalin rush she was feeling as she stretched and prepared for the race. 'I looked across at Marion. I had never seen her so nervous. She wasn't moving in her normal pre-race way, but she seemed jerky and jumpy. I think her nerves got to me a bit and I started to think about the finish and not the race.

'The very real possibility of winning the gold was speaking in my ears and I wasn't focusing on the actual race, just the result. But I genuinely believed it was my day to beat her in this race.'

Debbie's record in major championship finals reflects a progression of improvement. She saves her best and fastest time for the final. With this fact in mind, how does she explain her slower time in this one? 'When the gun went, I should have come out running as I normally do. In finals I get out and get into stride quickly, but this time I didn't. From this poor start, Marion was able to establish a lead because she got out quicker than I did. I had a lazy start, and after only 30 or 40 metres I knew I had blown my chance of the gold.'

Alpheus Finlayson, a former president of the Bahamas Amateur Athletic Association, has gone on record saying that Debbie did not chase Marion Jones enough in this race. He believes that she should have fought harder to catch the American.

Debbie agrees that she allowed Jones to get away, but explains, 'I felt disappointment as soon as we reached the 40-metre mark and I couldn't find that extra gear. I also know that if I dig too hard and too deep, I can lose form and relaxation. As a result, I don't run faster when I try harder.

'Sometimes it may not look as if I'm putting everything I have into a race but, believe me, I'm always trying. Then, when we came off the curve, I realised I was in danger of not even getting a medal and I was frightened it was going to be another Sydney. At that point I noticed Marion was breaking down a little too and losing some smoothness, so I really went all out for the finish and got second.'

Brent Stubbs, who lost his bet with the other sports reporters, nevertheless called Debbie's performance 'fantastic' and believes that this race marked the birth of a new, mature athlete. 'I have followed her career from school to college and into the professional arena, and I have witnessed the development, but I am convinced that this race moved her firmly into the realms of the great sprinters,' he explains.

After the race, when she had had time to reflect, Debbie was elated. 'Okay, it wasn't gold, but hey, it's a silver medal in the World Championships. It was my best ever individual performance. Of course I was happy. Marion's time in the final was the same as mine in the semi-final, so I know I could have taken first place, but I was very pleased with silver.'

The sequel to this event is related in the next chapter. The world now knows that following Marion Jones's confession about taking performance-enhancing drugs, Debbie was awarded the gold medal for this race.

Following a few more races in Europe at the end of the 2001 season, Debbie announced to the track and field world that she was leaving Elliott at the University of Georgia and would eventually move to Florida, much closer to her Bahamas home. She was going to join Amy Deem at the University of Miami.

She actually went to Miami on a whim: she had not even met Amy Deem before, although she knew of her record as a university coach. Debbie's manager suggested Deem and Debbie promptly took up the suggestion in January 2002.

Looking back at the years at Georgia and all she achieved, Debbie is reasonably satisfied with her accomplishments. There remains, however, a nagging thought in the back of her mind that occurs from time to time: what more might she have achieved if she had felt more confidence in her relationship with Elliott?

The difference in methods and personalities between Elliott and Deem was immediately obvious. Debbie felt a real sense of relief. In Miami, she felt free and relaxed, and responded positively to her new coach's methods. 'I found it much easier to work with her,' explains Debbie. Her ways took some adjusting to, but there was no hidden or not-so-hidden agenda with Coach Deem. She is quite stern, but I find her real and honest. She obviously enjoys what she does and communicates that enjoyment. I feel she is a technical coach.

'She is a real sprint specialist. She focuses on all the little details. We go over and over them until she is satisfied. I respect the way she coaches me, but I personally need the balance of the stamina running as well. I am so used to going the distance, I want to do the longer runs to warm up. Actually, I like the longer runs as a prologue to the short bursts.

'Coach Deem believes the stamina will come as a result of repetitions at high speed of the shorter bursts, concentrating on form, stride and all those other things we have to focus on.'

So, what is a day in the life of a professional athlete actually like? Debbie describes a typical training day: 'I get up around eight and eat. I like to have a good breakfast, because I won't be eating again until the evening and I'm going to be using up plenty of energy at the practice track. I make sure I pack bottles of water and other fluids and a snack to eat when the session is over.

'I will start with a warm-up for anywhere from 30 to 45 minutes. Coach Deem wants the warm-up period to be really active, so she has other exercise series built into it. It's very intense and by the time I finish warming up, I already feel tired.

'Coach Deem wants me to work on all parts of the body, so all my muscles are being used and it's continuous – there are no breaks between the exercises. After that come the drills: 30 metres running in a particular way. She might have me doing high knees or longer strides. There are a lot of different drills. I'll do two or three of this one, then two or three of another, and so on.

'Although it's only 30 metres at a time, I have to be aware of my form and technique. Coach Deem watches me like a hawk to check that I'm doing everything properly. Then, at last, we come to the sprint workout and, believe me, this can take for ever. She will have me doing sets of four sprints for 30 metres, 40 metres, 50 metres and 60 metres. Then there will be two at 80 metres and one last one at 90. 'I can rest between each individual sprint. I'll get a five-minute rest after each set of four. And I need that rest, I can tell you, because I have to do everything flat out so that Coach can see how I'm doing.

'Some days, the whole session can take from 11 in the morning until 4.30 in the afternoon. On a day like this, and training is not as intense as this every day, I have to work on any special aspect of my running as I'm doing these drills. If I want to fine-tune something to do with my start, for example, then I have to do it during the session.

'During the five-minute rest after each set, the coach and I will sit and talk. She will ask me how it felt and tell me what she has noticed. Sometimes she will have the video camera and we will watch the recording.

'She will point out anything she wants me to be aware of. Coach Deem is very thorough in this way and concentrates on the details of my style. I really like watching myself on the video, because it's so much easier to see what the coach is talking about if I can watch myself.

'As I said, not every day is like this: some are shorter. Some days I may concentrate on just one thing, and some days Coach Deem might make it a light, easy day.

'We have Sundays off, but work every other day. After the workouts on three days, we go into the weight room. This is very important, because it's the weight work that gives us our explosiveness. It's long and it's intense, and sometimes it hurts both physically and mentally. My muscles will be sore and I really don't want to do another set, but Coach Deem will outdo me and make me feel embarrassed, and I'll get on and do the rest.

'I always tell myself that I want to get better, that I want to be the best that I can be, so I will endure the pain to achieve that. When I've finished everything, I am exhausted and famished. That's why I pack a snack, so that I can eat something before going to have dinner.

'Before I finish completely, I stretch. Coach Deem doesn't believe in athletes stretching before the workout, but afterwards, when the muscles have done their work and are warm. There has been a reassessment of the value of stretching in the last few years and it seems that most coaches prefer their runners to stretch after they've warmed up. I know after a long flight I need to stretch, but I always get my muscles warm first these days in case I overstretch a tight muscle.'

By the time Debbie returns to her apartment in Miami, it will be getting dark. Most evenings she spends quietly, watching television or a film, recovering from the day's training.

We have seen how strong her focus is on her career: running has been her life. It may be different from many other occupations, with the quest for perfection involving physical and highly explosive activity, but Debbie quickly came to regard it as her job.

'The races and the championships give it the glamour and place me in the public eye,' she explains. 'The training days, however, are the bread and butter of an athlete's life. These are the days when the real work is done and the base is set for the competitive season.'

Does Debbie regard the racing and the competitions as work? 'Well, they're still part of my job. It's a bit like an actor, I suppose. The rehearsals are where the real work is done and the performance is the fun part. The races are my fun part. They are where the prize money comes from, so they're very much part of my job,' is how she rationalises it.

2002: success and recognition

Working with Amy Deem had an almost instant effect on Debbie's running and the 2002 season showed the results. Manchester, England, was the setting for the 17th Commonwealth Games. These games bring together athletes from most of the 71 countries that comprise the British Commonwealth. Although the event has lost some of its prestige since its inception, when it was second only to the Olympics, it is still a showpiece for athletes from Africa, the Caribbean, Australia, Canada, Britain and many other nations.

Debbie has always loved running in Britain: the people, she says, are highly knowledgeable about track and field, and come in their thousands to support the events.

Her performance certainly showed her enjoyment in running there. Entered for all her usual events, the 100 and 200 metres and the 4×100-metre relay, as usual, she thrived on it. The results speak for themselves: first in the final of the 100 metres, in a personal best time of 10.91 seconds; first in the final of the 200 metres, in a time of 22.20 seconds; first running the anchor leg in The Bahamas' relay team in 42.44 seconds. Three gold medals and three new Commonwealth Games records: outstanding achievements by any standards, and they easily won her the title of Outstanding Female Athlete of the Games.

'I did something at those games that I never imagined I would do,' recalls Debbie. 'I ran the fastest time of the year in the 200 and did my personal best in the 100, and it all felt so easy. I was flying and I never realised I was going so fast. Coach Deem's new methods really set me on the right track. This was the birth of a new Debbie Ferguson. I felt I could beat the world.'

Julie Wilson, Debbie's first sports teacher at secondary school and a member of the coaching staff for The Bahamas team at Manchester, provides probably the finest testimony to Debbie's performances at those games. 'I was on one of the shuttle buses going back into Manchester late one night towards the end of the games. I was sitting next to a young woman, who turned to me and we started to talk about the evening's races and events. I recognised her as Tessa Sanderson, the English javelin thrower who had won a gold medal in the 1984 Olympics in Los Angeles.

'She noticed my Bahamas team shirt and asked me if I knew Debbie. "Do I know her?" I said, "I once taught her!" Tessa was so complimentary about Debbie, commended her for the way she conducted herself on the track and in interviews, and couldn't say enough positive things about our Bahamas Golden Girl. Coming from such a talented and highly respected former champion, those comments really made me feel good for Debbie and for The Bahamas.'

From Manchester, Debbie went to Madrid as a member of the Americas team to compete in the IAAF World Cup. This is a regional event and in 2002 attracted teams representing the Americas, the United States, Oceania, Europe, Asia, Africa, Germany, Russia and the host nation, Spain. Debbie was selected for the 200 metres and the 4×100-metre relay. She achieved what no other Bahamian athlete has ever done before or since, by winning an individual gold medal. She tore up the Madrid track in the 200 metres, winning by a comfortable three-tenths of a second from Muriel Hurtis of France. In the relay, she teamed up with three Jamaican friends from the international circuit, Beverly McDonald, Juliet Campbell and Tayna Lawrence, and ran the anchor leg.

The Americas team was trailing the United States when Debbie took the baton, but she chased down Gail Devers over the final leg and brought her team to victory in a world best time for 2002 of 41.91 seconds.

'The summer of 2002 was a special one for me and I relished every minute of it,' is how she describes her summer of triumph. 'The sports journalists then voted me Female Athlete of the Year, so I returned to Nassau on top of the world. Life plays some funny tricks, however, because shortly after I got back, I broke up with my fiancé, George.

'I was devastated for a while, because it happened out of the blue. In spite of the separations, we had maintained our relationship for something like 12 years, and had been friends for even longer. I never imagined this would happen. It was very ironic, coming just after such a great season, but I have learned to look at life philosophically. I always try to see the best of a situation and that's what I did. I can't dwell on the negative. Life is too short.'

Fate soon produced another surprise for Debbie, although this time a very pleasant one. Out of the blue, she learned that she had been selected as a Goodwill Ambassador for the FAO (the Food and Agriculture Organization of the United Nations). The FAO leads international efforts to defeat hunger. Serving both developed and developing countries, it acts as a neutral forum where all nations meet as equals to negotiate agreements and debate policy. The FAO is also a source of knowledge and information. It helps developing countries and countries in transition to modernise and improve their agricultural, forestry and fisheries practices, with the long-term aim of ensuring good nutrition for all.

Since its founding in 1945, it has focused special attention on developing rural areas, where 70 per cent of the world's poor and hungry live. Debbie believes that her involvement in The Bahamas with underprivileged people led to such an honour, which she regards as her greatest to date. 'I was so surprised,' Debbie admits, 'but it was extremely gratifying to be recognised as having this sort of role to play on a world stage. I believe we should not only treasure what we have now. We should also help others obtain what they should have.'

Debbie and her mother travelled to the headquarters of the FAO in Rome for her investiture as an ambassador on World Food Day, 2002. Also joining the list of ambassadors on that day was the African American singer, Dionne Warwick, who Debbie describes as 'one of the most beautiful women I have ever met. It was a very memorable experience to be there and to meet such a famous and respected woman, who is appreciated all over the world. I sat next to her at the round-table discussion and she is just an awesome lady.

'I also met the president of Venezuela, who invited me to go to his country on behalf of FAO and begin a plan he had been putting together with the United Nations. Unfortunately, it never happened because of political unrest, so that's still one country I've never visited.

'I was also happy that my mom could be there with me to share in the occasion and to visit and see the city of Rome. I owe her so much, so I felt I was beginning to repay her in a small way for all she did when I was a girl.'

Debbie found herself on a list of ambassadors that includes such notable names as Dee Dee Bridgewater, the African American jazz singer; Carla Fracci, world-famous Italian ballerina; Raúl González, striker for the Real Madrid soccer team and the highest scorer of goals in the Spanish national team's history; Mory Kanté, one of West Africa's most celebrated singers; Miriam Makeba, Mama Africa, South Africa's most renowned singer and humanitarian activist; Oumou Sangaré, the leading female singer from Mali and a fighter for women's rights in that part of the world; Gina Lollobrigida, the legendary Italian film star; and Youssou N'Dour, the world-famous Senegalese singer. Heady company indeed!

In her speech of acceptance, Debbie said, 'It is indeed an honour to be here on this special occasion. I would like to thank the Food and Agricultural Organization of the United Nations for such a prestigious and distinct role, which I graciously accept. I take pleasure in winning gold medals; however, it would be more gratifying for me to see the FAO capture the gold medal against hunger. I should like to take this opportunity to thank the organising committee for giving a young lady of my nature and status a chance to represent FAO. Now, let us get excited and rejuvenate to work a little harder in order to win this race against hunger. Through commitment, dedication and hard work we can make this dream a reality.' She was warmly applauded as she returned to her seat.

'I firmly believe in the ideals of FAO,' she says. 'They want to eradicate hunger, not by giving people a fish to eat, but by teaching them how to catch fish. I like that approach.

'Since that time, I have been to Andros (the largest of the Bahamian islands) to encourage the Androsians to develop their farming industry and to speak about sustaining the resources of the land. FAO has also sponsored some farming projects there and I observed what was happening with them. I plan to do more in this region in 2006.

'If anyone had suggested to me back in Westmoreland when I was chasing around my grandparents' yard that something like this was going to happen to me, I would have scoffed at the idea. But it's happened and it's all part of the fairy tale.'

Adrian

Back home in Nassau for a rest, Debbie realised that, following the break-up with George, she could no longer use George's car as she had used to. She wanted to establish a new image for herself following the events of the year, so she went to a dealership advertising Japanese jeeps. Assisting her that day was a tall, well-built young man, who impressed her with his honesty and the care he took to explain the features of the car. His name was Adrian McKenzie.

Debbie reveals, 'I'm not sure what it was exactly, but I found myself thinking about this man a lot. He must have been thinking about me too, because he ended up calling me and we went out. There was a special feeling about our relationship and we soon started "going steady".'

In 2005, Debbie said, 'We are now engaged and plan to marry just before Christmas. He is able to accept my lifestyle, which means I will not be with him for a large part of each year. We have built up an implicit trust in each other. It's all going very well, I'm pleased to say.'

On the European tour

In 2003, a second tattoo appeared on Debbie's other leg, to accompany the horse drawn when she was on the University of Georgia track team. This one bore the word 'relentless', the same word that Adrian has tattooed on his neck. Debbie explains the significance: 'I liked Adrian's. When he showed me the definition in his dictionary, I thought it applied to me – "not giving up, being determined, always giving your all".

'So I thought I would have the word put on my leg, where it would only be seen when I run. I had the horse on the other leg done while I was at Georgia. All the track team were getting them. They urged me to get one too. I said, "No, my mom will kill me," but they persuaded me.'

After 1999, Debbie spent the summer months competing on the European circuit. She participated in all the prestigious meets, from Bislet to Brussels and Helsinki to Rome, and was also able to indulge her passion for seeing new countries.

Europe is where the world's best athletes gravitate to each summer to compete in the Golden League, the Grand Prix series and the World Athletic Gala. Competition begins long before the athletes actually step onto the track, because agents and managers will try to persuade the meet promoters that their athletes should be invited. Debbie's manager, Ray Flynn of Flynn Sports Management, would be involved in lengthy negotiations all through the summer, ensuring that she was able to run at the best meets.

Debbie explained at the time, 'I'm happy to leave all the arrangements to Ray, because I just wouldn't have the time. He makes sure the airline tickets are there and that the promoters are expecting me. If I'm running the times, then he will be able to get me into the meets.

'Now that my name is out there, I don't have any trouble being accepted, but it wasn't quite so straightforward in the early days. I can remember going to meets and thinking I was running in the 100 metres, and finding out the day before the race that maybe a local runner was replacing me because her presence would add to the attendance.

'Other times, I found myself bumped from a race because another agent had brought a group of runners, including a big name like Maurice Green or Marion Jones, so one of his other, lesser-known runners was going to run in my place. That sort of thing goes on all the time because the promoters want to make as much money as they can.'

With usually at least one meet each week, there was a lot of travel. Debbie grew accustomed to living out of a suitcase and wearing a tracksuit for almost the entire summer. She would try to establish a routine for these meets: 'We try to get to the meet at least one day in advance, so we can familiarise ourselves with the surroundings. I say "we" because the athletes normally travel together. I prefer to go straight to the hotel, but sometimes the promoters have arranged a function for us to attend before we get the chance to unwind.

'The best of these are the camps we do at the tracks with the schoolchildren. In Europe, the schools really promote track. The kids come out in their hundreds when international runners are in town. I love talking to them and giving them tips. Sometimes, we can actually do some work with them and watch them run.

'But often we just take a few pictures and sign autographs. This can take a long time when there are sometimes over 500 youngsters in attendance. I can spend over an hour signing autographs because I hate to disappoint anyone.

'I remember a time when I was still very young when I asked Gwen Torrence, one of my sprinting idols, for her autograph. She wouldn't sign. I was so disillusioned and upset. So I don't want any young person to feel the way I did at that time. I will always do my best to sign for everyone. Most of these youngsters are very appreciative.

'I realise that if we want track and field to continue and to grow, we must encourage the children. Even though we may be in countries where the children don't speak English, these kids are very, very receptive.'

Track and field has a much higher profile in Europe than it does in the US, despite all the money invested in American university track programmes. European television channels show track meets live throughout the summer months and the papers carry athletics stories daily. This is why the European season developed and why it is the hub of the track world from June to September.

Debbie's most regular roommate in Europe was Savatheda Fynes, her relay teammate. 'We get along really well,' related Debbie, 'and we are best friends. She can put up with my little foibles and I can take her little idiosyncrasies. Whenever Savatheda is on the tour with me, we room together.'

For her own part, Savatheda said, 'Debbie is my best friend in the track world. We have got along very well since we used to run in high school. She is the most friendly person you can ever meet. She always wants to stop and talk to everyone. I've been telling her for a long time that she should pay more attention to herself, because sometimes she spends so much time talking to people at the track and signing autographs that she has no time for herself. But that's just her. She finds it so hard to say no to anyone.'

Debbie and Savatheda were rivals in Olympic finals, as well as in races on the European tour, but their rivalry would disappear as soon as the races were over. 'Even in the big races,' said Savatheda, 'we will be talking about all kinds of foolishness right up to the time the starter says, "Take your marks." Then we get serious for about a minute, and after that we're back to joking and laughing again.'

At home in Nassau, Debbie's timekeeping is constantly put at risk by her involvement with different projects and her keenness to satisfy everyone with whom she comes into contact. Meetings or engagements frequently overrun, and she is often late for her afternoon or evening commitments.

Savatheda explains how this contrasted with Debbie's approach when travelling. 'She is never late on the tour. She's actually highly organised and tidy. I have to tell her not to rearrange my things because she has an obsession with turning all the labels so you can read them: bottles, jars, soaps. You name it, Debbie wants the label the right way round. It's just one of her habits.'

Debbie mocks herself over this habit, but she is not able to do anything about it. She has always been a tidy person and taken responsibility for cleaning the houses and apartments she has lived in. 'At home and on the tour, I like to have the labels the right way round.'

If Savatheda was not there, Debbie would always looks for another Bahamian competitor as her roommate. If she was the only Bahamian, she would share with one of the Jamaican women or someone from the US.

'I don't like to share with one of my opponents. I find it a little awkward to share a room with a woman and then go out and race against her. They admit to finding it uncomfortable too. A young Bahamian 400-metre specialist, Christine Amertil, is one of my newest roommates, and another, who I have been rooming with off and on for years, is Jackie Edwards. Jackie is great to share with because we have similar senses of humour and we laugh together nearly all the time.'

Jackie shares Debbie's views: 'We room together and spend the whole night laughing. Debbie is very open, frank and honest, and we communicate well together.' Jackie, an experienced long jumper, had been on the scene even longer, but valued Debbie's friendship and truly enjoyed her company.

In this way, the summer season would develop. The athletes would be taken care of by the meet promoters while they were in a city, but they had to look after their own financial arrangements, their own cellphones and their own dietary needs if they did not want the food provided. 'The hospitality varies from meet to meet,' Debbie said. 'Sometimes we have so much to eat we have to refuse some. Other times there is barely enough to survive on. Also, we sometimes arrive in a place exhausted, especially if we travel from the previous meet on the same night we competed. I'm always so high after I race that it's impossible to sleep if we travel immediately. So I arrive bleary-eyed and weary the next day.'

When athletes travel from meet to meet in Europe, there might be a group of them on the same plane or in the same bus. There is a strong camaraderie – it is like a large family. 'Athletes from the Caribbean countries naturally congregate together,' Debbie explains. 'And the US athletes tend to travel together, too. We all get on pretty well off the track. It is business when we're racing, but when we're travelling from city to city, we're good friends.'

As the European tour nears its end, there is great interest in discovering who is invited to the World Athletic Gala in Monte Carlo. Debbie went on two occasions and it was one of her favourite meets. 'It's a great way to end the season. Although we're all weary, we all find a little bit extra for Monte Carlo,' Debbie said.

In the Gala of September 2004, there was a fascinating rematch from the 200-metre final of the Athens Olympics, when Debbie found herself running against her good friend and Athens gold medallist, Veronica Campbell.

Again, Debbie was criticised for not attacking the favourite hard enough from the gun. She admits that she started too gently. 'By the time I got into full stride there was too much to do to catch Veronica, but I closed to within 0.02 of a second by the finish. If I had gone out like I did in Athens, I think I would have beaten her,' she acknowledged.

Debbie often talks about the fatigue that she feels during training and as the season progresses. For some people it is difficult to grasp that races that last just over 11 seconds, or just over 22 for the 200 metres, can cause such tiredness.

Debbie talks about the very high level of focus and concentration required, the intense marshalling of all her energies and strength into those short bursts of speed, and the nervous energy and high levels of adrenalin that are pumped around her body every time she competes.

She confesses to feeling elated but exhausted when a race is over, in the same way as a distance runner feels after a long race. Those who still find it hard to accept that sprinters exhaust themselves running 100 metres should also consider the fact that all runners train for their specialty events. All their preparation is directed towards their own distance. Consequently, when they perform to their limits, they will expend just as much energy as someone who trains for a longer event. When the travelling is taken into account, and extra transatlantic journeys to special meets at home and in the US, it is not difficult to empathise with claims of fatigue.

Down, but certainly not out

All professional athletes fear the spectre of a career-ending injury. Ever since the mysterious lower-back problem in Georgia in 1997, Debbie has been concerned about injuries and their effect.

She is grateful for having been injury-free for most of her professional career, although in 2003 she suffered a severe ankle tear, which completely destroyed her season. The disappointment was acute, as her preparations for the World Championships in Paris had begun so well. 'I ran the world's fastest 100 metres in South Africa, 10.97 seconds, early in my build-up and was feeling very confident,' she recalls. 'I was strong and ready. Then, one day in training, I felt this odd sort of pain in my ankle and I couldn't run. I lost my spring and my speed. I was told to rest for a month. That month was like purgatory, because I was just itching to be on the track. Before the injury, I was running better than ever. Then this setback came along.

'After the month's rest, I started working again, but I returned to competition too soon. After the rest, the injury wasn't bad enough to stop me running, but it was bad enough to stop me producing my best form.

'I went to the World Championships, but it was a disaster. I didn't make the finals in either the 100 or the 200 metres, which was not only disappointing, but is unheard of for me. It felt as if my foot was just flopping around like a fish on a line. I had no power or real balance. So I had to take the rest of the season off. The injury was actually worse than I thought, because it took until March of 2004 before I was completely free of it.'

The injury meant that 2003 was a bleak year, in terms of both results and finances. But the gods had another twist in store for her after the World Championships.

During the competition, all the affiliated athletes were asked to vote for their official representatives on the IAAF Athletes' Commission. There were 26 nominations. The 12 with the most votes were selected to serve on the commission for four years. Debbie received 633 votes, the third highest total. She was beaten only by two kings of the track, Ethiopian Haile Gebrselassie and Moroccan Hicham El Guerrouj, both the recipients of multiple gold medals and worldwide household names. Paula Radcliffe, the British marathon and 10,000-metre specialist, was also one of the 12 selected.

To have been thus selected by her peers of the international athletics world is a true testament to the esteem in which Debbie is

179

held by other competitors. Her personality, humility and amiability make her an ideal choice for the position. Her instinctive desire to see fair play for all, coupled with her ability to speak persuasively and lucidly make her all the more qualified to act on behalf of her peers and fellow athletes.

2004: surgery

When the ankle injury finally cleared up in the spring of 2004, Debbie was still troubled by some occasionally acute abdominal pains. She was told that she was suffering from fibroids and surgery would be needed. 'I couldn't have the surgery then, with the Olympics so close, so I chose to wait until after the season,' Debbie explains.

Given the successes she enjoyed in 2004, it was probably a good decision, but during July, August and September she suffered serious bouts of pain, especially during her monthly cycle, when the bleeding persisted for two weeks at a time. 'I was worried about becoming anaemic,' states Debbie, 'and I prayed that the period would not come while I was racing in Athens. All was well for the 100, but it came for the 200 and I was in considerable pain for all the 200-metre heats and the final. I was determined not to let the pain spoil my chances and, thankfully, it didn't.'

However, when she eventually returned to Nassau, she knew she could not delay the surgery any longer and made the necessary arrangements to have the operation early in October. 'I had a feeling the fibroids had become worse, but I wasn't prepared for what the surgeon told me afterwards. They removed 12 fibroids! I was so stiff and felt so weak that I had to rest for weeks and could not start my foundation work in November, as I usually do, but had to wait until returning to Miami in January.'

The prolonged rest left Debbie frustrated, but it did allow her to recharge her batteries. By the time she began serious training with Coach Deem, she felt very strong and in exactly the right frame of mind to prepare for the next World Championships, in Helsinki.

'My severed abdominal muscles needed a lot of work, but I was making good progress when I suffered another setback,' relates Debbie. 'One day, after training, I suddenly fell down in the most excruciating pain I have ever felt. I was in agony and my stomach was becoming distended. I vomited, yet my stomach was sticking right out. I felt hungry, but I couldn't eat.

'I rushed to the emergency room and, when I explained about the fibroids surgery, they opened me up again. They discovered two blockages in my intestinal tract, caused by scar tissue from the removal of the fibroids. They were able to clear the blockages and they also removed my appendix. They reasoned that I was probably going to need to have it taken out at some time – most athletes do, apparently – and they didn't think my abdominal region could take a third major incision.'

Debbie has felt fine since the surgery, but the impossibility of restarting training in time meant that she had to miss the entire 2005 season. This meant that she would have to forego the World Championships, and would also be unavailable to run for The Bahamas in the Senior CAC Games to be hosted in Nassau over The Bahamas independence weekend. The latter was a huge disappointment, not just for Debbie, but for all her fans in The Bahamas, none of whom had had the opportunity to see her run for her country on home territory since the 1992 CARIFTA Games.

An inspiration to all

Debbie attended the CAC Games, but as a commentator for Island 102.9, a local radio station. On her way round the stadium, she would be stopped every couple of strides to sign autographs or to pose for a photo with a child. She would be accosted by other athletes from all the different countries, seeking advice or simply wishing to greet her. She would be approached by old friends, acquaintances and people she had never met before, all inquiring about her health and passing on good wishes.

The remarkable thing is that now, as then, she stops, talks, poses, signs or listens with as much interest for the persons she does not know as for those who are old friends. Nothing seems to be too much trouble and everybody is worthy of her full attention.

Missing the World Championships affected Debbie's relationship with her kit sponsor, Adidas. In 2004, they were working on a shoe specially designed for Debbie to wear in Helsinki. 'It was such a pretty design. The shoes were aqua, but the three Adidas stripes were in yellow and black, so they had all three colours of the Bahamian flag. I was so looking forward to wearing them.'

Adidas have been very generous with sportswear to Debbie over the years. When her ex-fiancé, George, started his own track club, Bahamas Speed Dynamics, Debbie donated much of the Adidas clothing to the club members, who wore it proudly. While she was never officially part of George's club, she would go to the track regularly to help in the training and give words of encouragement.

George was grateful for her presence: 'Debbie's being there gave the club a higher profile, particularly when we were just getting started. The kit and the shoes were added bonuses that inspired my runners,' he explains.

Debbie's relationship with George is still cordial, and her genuine interest in his club and the successes of its members still takes her to watch practices. She says, 'I will always take an interest in our young people working on the track. It helped me so much and gave me so many opportunities that I try to encourage as many kids as possible to do their best and make their dreams come true.'

That is the message that Debbie regularly repeats in the months between September and Christmas each year, when she is back home in Nassau. When so many sporting heroes seem to be destroying their own images, Debbie's lifestyle and involvement in charity work stand as a benchmark for all that is positive for young people to follow. Publicly, she has been used to advertise various products and The Bahamas' cable TV company, Cable Bahamas, has her face on many of its vans and trucks, so she is constantly visible.

The Bahamas Amateur Athletic Association often uses her in official meetings, and she was included in the organising body of the 2005 CAC Games in Nassau. The Bahamas Olympic Committee invited her to be one of the baton carriers for the ceremonial journey of the stick for the 2006 Commonwealth Games in Melbourne.

Debbie's role in the FAO led to a full-page advertisement in *National Geographic* magazine, in February 2005. A close-up of Debbie was captioned with the text, 'If you think hunger is a problem that should have been wiped out years ago … you're not the only one.' Her public profile is such that the organisations with which she is associated know that she will not let them down and that they can rely on her integrity as a role model.

Alpheus Finlayson explains it like this: 'What makes the difference between Debbie and everybody else is her personality. Debbie has never been the top athlete in the world, but the people involved in the sport have placed her on a pedestal higher than almost all others. A combination of her ability and her friendliness and concern for others makes her very special.'

Brent Stubbs tells of times in stadiums all over the world when Debbie would leave the track and walk through the athletes' tunnel to meet the press: 'She never refuses an interview and always explains in as much detail as she can. The foreign journalists love talking to her because she will tell them about The Bahamas and living here, as well as talking about the races and her own performances. She can put on a show for the reporters without being false. In fact, she gives such good interviews because she is so honest and never fake.'

The Debbie we see in such public places, however, is not the complete story. Every year, between September and December, she involves herself in what she calls 'giving back' to the community. This takes her to a number of Nassau's schools to speak at assemblies, to the children's homes to spend time with the children and give advice, to the old people's homes to sit and listen and to enjoy their company, and to all sorts of events such as parties, sports meets and church outings.

'I have seen this as my mission ever since I went to Georgia. I went there, but I grew up in the ghetto. I try to convince our Bahamian young people that it's not where you come from, but where you want to go that is important,' is how Debbie explains it.

She is in a unique position because she can relate personally to so many of the problems and difficulties that young people face, and they respond to her because they sense she is genuine and believes in her own message.

In Nassau, there is a home for orphaned children and children whose parents, for whatever reasons, cannot take care of them. It is called the Ranfurly Homes for Children. Debbie has often visited, but remembers one visit in particular: 'I spent the whole afternoon talking with the girls. They didn't want me to leave. I had to go, but I promised I would come back and I would spend the night.

'I don't think they believed me, but I was determined to do it. So, at the first opportunity, I went back with my bag of night clothes and I stayed the night.

'We didn't sleep much though. The girls were so thrilled that they stayed up all night talking with me. They were saying things like, "I can't believe you actually stayed the night here," but they were so appreciative. We talked about everything. They responded sincerely because they could tell I was sincere.

'I always tell children to do their best in school and to follow their dreams. It's a simple message, but it's workable if you're determined. I want young people to know where I grew up and the kind of life I had as a child. I impress upon them that if I could do it, so can they.'

Debbie tries to dismantle the superstar image that many young people have of her by demonstrating that she is as human as they are. She takes great pride in the knowledge that some of the children from Ranfurly have won scholarships to private schools since she spoke to them. She recalls one occasion: 'One of the girls actually showed me a 1 dollar bill I had signed for her years ago. She had kept it and told me she had used it as inspiration over the years. In 2002, the year I met her, she won a scholarship to Nassau's private Kingsway Academy.'

Debbie remembers another day when she was recording a promotional commercial for the CAC Games outside the offices of the major sponsor, Colina Insurance. A woman leaving the building recognised her: 'My niece, Coeryce,' she said, 'did a project and wrote a poem about you at school. She admires you so much. Will you visit her school and speak to the children?'

'Of course, I couldn't say no,' relates Debbie. 'I went to the school, Garvin Tynes Primary. The children were wonderful: so mannerly and so polite. And the little girl's poem was so sweet. She didn't know me. We hadn't met, but it was so accurate. She gave me a copy and I have kept it at home.'

There are often chance meetings that turn into great experiences. Debbie feels a great sense of satisfaction and accomplishment in her relations with the young as a result. One Saturday, she was at the track stadium for a photo shoot. There was a small meet going on, organised by the Baptist Churches in Nassau for their young people. Only a handful of competitors attended, but medals were presented after the events and the event was given as much ceremony as possible, to honour the winners.

When the photo shoot was over, Debbie walked across to the presentation area and was immediately surrounded by the children. She was asked by the organisers if she would present some of the medals. She readily agreed and once again seized the chance to speak encouragingly to the winners. 'Congratulations,' she told them. 'But make sure you try to get As in your school work. Then you can get a scholarship to college.'

In this way, she is able to turn a chance meeting into a special occasion. She does it with an ease and a style that are as impressive to watch as they are natural. 'I always talk from my heart. It's the only way I know how. Sometimes when I tell kids about my life, they look absolutely amazed.

'They see that I made something of myself by working hard, staying focused, having a clear goal and not letting negative things hold me back. I believe in children. I want them to believe that they can play a part in the world out there and they don't have to break the law to do it. These children of all ages in all sorts of different schools listen to me. As a result, I believe it's my calling to motivate them. If I can touch the life of one child in a positive and meaningful way, it gives me a priceless sense of accomplishment.'

She often returns to St Andrew's School, her alma mater. On one very special occasion, she returned as guest speaker at the graduation ceremony for the class of 2001. It was the first graduating class after Debbie's gold medal in Sydney and she spoke eloquently about the importance of developing the right attitude for success in life.

'I was very nervous about that speech because it was St Andrew's, with all its really smart students. I wanted to pitch it at a level that would challenge them. Normally, I speak without a script, but for that graduation I had it all written out, word for word.'

Another visit to St Andrew's occurred shortly after her return to Nassau in 2004 and she took her bronze medal with her. 'It was a great day,' reflects Debbie, 'but I couldn't help noticing a young student in a wheelchair at the back. I went to speak to her. I discovered that her name was Jade. She had been involved in a car accident that had taken the life of one of her peers at the school two years before. She was now trying to resume her studies, but was not able to do very much and could not walk.

'I felt for her. I admired her courage. So I took some pictures with her and she gave me her phone number. I called her a while later. I took her shopping to Bay Street. I wanted to show her I respected the way she was trying to cope with her disability. I wanted to encourage her not to give up.'

A small gesture, maybe, but Debbie makes them constantly. Even when her calendar is full, she will still try to fit in one more visit or stop to sign another autograph. Moreover, she has never forgotten the people who have been instrumental in helping her and guiding her since childhood. She will always make time while she is in Nassau to visit Ms Lockhart, Mrs Nesbeth, Mrs Bethel, Mr Rahming, people from her church, old friends from school and former neighbours.

Helsinki 2005

Unable to compete after her second major abdominal surgery in six months, Debbie found the summer of 2005 frustrating: 'I have been asked to help the BAAA with some projects. I worked at the CAC Games, but it's nothing like actually being on the track competing. I'm grateful to be involved in some way at least. The IAAF invited me to attend the World Championships in Helsinki in my role as athlete representative. They asked me to survey the other athletes about some issues like the new false start rule. Between that and my advisory role for the Bahamas team, I was very busy, but I wish I had been there to run.'

While in Helsinki, Debbie shared a room with fellow Bahamian and her old Georgia teammate, Tonique Williams-Darling, who was hoping to complete the double of winning a World Championship gold medal to accompany the Olympic gold she won in Athens. This was the first time they had roomed together at a major championship and, although Debbie was concerned that she might distract Tonique from her preparations, it actually turned out to be extremely beneficial for Tonique.

'Tonique was extremely focused, but she was also more stressed than I have seen her for some time,' explains Debbie, who thoroughly enjoyed rooming with her old friend. 'We reminisced about the old days in Georgia. I believe my presence there in the room helped her to relax. I wrote her a note before she started in the heats for the 400 metres to help calm her nerves and relieve the pressure. She taped it above her bed so she could take inspiration from it each day.

'I felt proud and special knowing that she used the note so openly to give her inspiration. Basically, I encouraged her to get going, because she had trodden this familiar road before. She knew she could do it. She just needed to be reminded.

'I believed in her. I was overjoyed when she made history and won the gold on that cold, rainy night in Finland. Now she is our first female individual gold medallist on the track in the Olympics and in the World Championships.'

Debbie kept herself busy in Helsinki and encouraged and helped as many of The Bahamas team as she could. 'There were also commiserations to express,' she confesses, 'especially to the women's 4×100-metre relay team, who had high hopes for a medal, but sadly didn't finish their heat. Chandra was jostled just as she was about to start moving for the first changeover and fell over. Our first runner, Tameka Clarke, could only stare in disbelief as she had nobody to hand the baton to. And then there was Jackie Edwards' disappointment. She missed making the final of the long jump by one centimetre! Those two near misses show what a fine line there is sometimes between success and failure.

'I couldn't help thinking how I would have felt if that jostling accident had happened to Chandra in the Sydney Olympics. Our whole lives might have been different.'

The world of track and field

In spite of her involvement with The Bahamas team in Helsinki, Debbie's most vivid memories of that World Championships

189

involved events off the track. Debbie was privileged to meet many legendary former champions visiting the championships.

'There were too many to list, but I was so proud to meet some of the greatest champions of all time,' she enthused. 'The amazing thing was that most of them recognised me and asked me about my injury and how I was doing. Edwin Moses, Don Quarrie, Bert Cameron and Grace Jackson were there, and I met them all. Others, who were just names from the past before I went to Helsinki – Kipchoge Keino, Lasse Virén and Valeri Borzov, who were great Olympic champions – are now almost my friends. And then I met a very special person, Austin Sealy, the Barbadian champion, whose name graces the CARIFTA award I won in 1995 as outstanding athlete of the games. It was a great honour to meet him.'

Nevertheless, in spite of coming into contact with all these remarkable former champions, there is one ex-champion whom Debbie holds in far higher esteem than anyone else in the track and field world. Jonathan Edwards, the former British triple jumper, was also in Helsinki, working for the BBC as a commentator. Debbie chatted with him between his commentaries. 'He has been an idol of mine – my greatest idol really – for a long time,' explained Debbie. 'I admired his approach, his humility and the great ambassador's job he has always done for track and field. His record as an athlete speaks for itself. He was a world champion, an Olympic champion and a world record holder, but as a person he is just fantastic.'

Debbie recalls one occasion some years ago when she was struggling with all her bags on her way to catch a flight to Stockholm. Jonathan Edwards was checking in for the same flight. Debbie's luggage was over the maximum weight and she was about to be charged a large sum for the excess. Edwards, who recognised Debbie as a fellow competitor, offered to take her extra bag for her and carried it all the way to the plane.

'I knew who he was,' says Debbie, 'but we had never spoken before. So for him to do such a generous and kind thing for me immediately elevated him in my mind. I knew he was a Christian at the time, and I had always respected him for his stance on not competing on Sundays. But at that moment I came to know what a humane person he was. He is so approachable and very considerate of other people.'

It is a truism that we tend to be attracted to people who either demonstrate characteristics that we would like to exemplify ourselves or who manifest positive characteristics that we feel we embody ourselves. Debbie's respect for Jonathan Edwards can be classified in either category: she certainly carries herself with the same generosity of spirit and humility and is herself a very humane person.

The plight of the poor and the problems that afflict the poorer countries of the world have concerned Debbie for a long time now. In 2004, she approached the IAAF with an idea for fund-raising to help the people in those countries. Her idea was turned down at the time, but someone at the IAAF kept it in mind and a charity event called 'Athletics for a Better World' was started. Debbie was chosen to be one of its five ambassadors, representing the five main areas of the world. She joined Beatrice Faumuina, former world champion discus thrower from New Zealand; Carolina Klüft, world heptathlon champion from Sweden; Koji Murofushi, Athens Olympic gold medal hammer thrower from Japan; and Paul Tergat, world record holder in the marathon from Kenya. Debbie spent many hours in Helsinki, working on behalf of Athletes for A Better World, gathering donations from athletes to be used at the end of the year in a major fund-raising auction.

'I managed to get Allyson Felix, the world champion at 200 metres, to donate her spikes. I persuaded Justin Gatlin, the world and Olympic champion at 100 metres, to give his running uniform. Tonique Williams, my friend and roommate, gave her Bahamas uniform. My training partner and world champion in the 100 metres, Lauryn Williams, signed and donated her US uniform. The Bahamas men's 4×400 relay team donated a signed tracksuit jacket, and many other athletes from the Caribbean and the US, who were my responsibility, gave items that they autographed for the auction,' explains Debbie.

'It was very gratifying for me to see how willingly the athletes gave and supported this initiative.' Debbie hoped that the online auction at the end of the year would raise about a million dollars for UNICEF and other world organisations to help fight poverty.

Another important issue that concerns Debbie, and one that has simmered in the track and field world throughout her career, is illegal performance-enhancing drug use among athletes. There is no doubt that her sport has been tainted by instances, or accusations, of using banned substances, in some cases by world and Olympic champions.

Debbie is vehemently opposed to all forms of drug taking, even if she has not been as openly critical of the drug cheats as British long-distance runner, Paula Radcliffe, who draped a banner denouncing one of her rivals over the perimeter wall of the track at one major championship for all the world to see.

Debbie keeps her remarks private. 'I believe in fair competition – runner against runner – not runner against runner plus some unnatural additive. I grew up in the church. My belief and spiritual strength come from faith. To me, drug taking is cheating. I believe that those who do it are not only cheating other runners, but are ultimately cheating themselves. I wonder what they will be thinking years down the road when they take stock of themselves and look honestly at who they are.'

Debbie says that the clean runners are all aware of athletes who take 'the stuff'. But she has never even been tempted to indulge in it herself. She cannot see the point. She reasons, 'Of course it's nice to win the medals. But where is the value of a medal won by cheating? I couldn't look people – my benefactors, the children I deal with, my friends in The Bahamas team and, more importantly, myself – in the face if I succumbed to taking drugs.'

What is it, then, that causes athletes to start taking drugs? Debbie is convinced it starts with the coaches. 'We all know who the drug coaches are. They are desperate for the reflected glory of coaching a world champion or world record holder. They convince their athletes that there's nothing wrong with taking them.

'I've never been offered drugs *per se*, but I have been approached by coaches whose reputations are murky, to say the least, to train with them. But I've never been tempted, because I know what that would mean.

'We've all seen what happens. Someone takes the stuff, almost immediately starts beating us and wins a gold medal somewhere. Then, a matter of only a few days later, when she is no longer taking it, she will get beaten by the rest of us. I regard it as selling your soul. I would never do it.'

Some people have put forward the idea that the drugs should be available to all and the bans lifted. In this way, the playing field would be levelled and there would be greater equality. Debbie discounts the idea, because there are so many athletes like her who simply do not want to take drugs.

'It's not only the moral reasons, but there are the health concerns too; so many of these designer substances have not been fully tested. Who knows what damage they are causing?

'Look at what happened to some of those East German women years ago. They were forced to take substances when they were competing. When they stopped and wanted to have children, they either couldn't or gave birth to babies with terrible defects. But that can be the price you have to pay.'

Debbie wonders how athletes escape detection, because there are stringent tests after races. She thinks that the drug makers have become very sophisticated, but also that the testers don't know what they're searching for much of the time.

'New, modified versions of the drugs seem to be appearing all the time,' she explains. 'Very often they can't be detected because the testing equipment can't identify it. Racing, sprinting especially, is such a basic sport. People running to see who is fastest – it's a fundamental challenge. It doesn't need all this drug stuff.'

Making a living

In six seasons as a professional athlete, Debbie succeeded in making a reasonable living. She has enjoyed some substantial prizes that have offset the bleak year in 2003 and the completely barren one in 2005. She has been able to build a small apartment duplex to the east of Nassau and a house in a government housing project not too far away from her first school in Oakes Field. This is her pride and joy, born out of her desire to have a comfortable house of her own and one in which her mother, the source of so much of her inspiration and support, can live happily and in comfort.

'I've managed to achieve some things,' Debbie explained in 2005, 'but you must remember that the expenses of my sporting life are very high too. My manager, air fares, my coach, all drain my resources, and medical bills have been enormous over the last three years. I receive a stipend from The Bahamas government, but it doesn't go very far. I cannot get medical insurance. Once they hear I'm an athlete, the insurance companies back right off. Don't get me wrong now, I wouldn't change my life, but sometimes it's very expensive.'

Expensive or not, Debbie went to Helsinki and worked tirelessly in the background for the IAAF and The Bahamas team. She used her ability to communicate with and inspire the younger members of her country's team. She accomplished it wholeheartedly, in the way she does everything else.

While there, she naturally felt disappointed at not being able to join her teammates on the track, but she looked beyond Helsinki and focused on the next set of challenges – challenges that were to begin in September 2005, when she broke her normal routine and returned to Miami to work with Coach Deem, to rebuild her shattered abdominal muscles and to lay the foundation for the 2006 season.

She had an added incentive in that one of her training partners, American Lauryn Williams, won the individual gold medal in the women's 100 metres at the Helsinki World Championships.

'When we're training together,' explained Debbie, 'I can never let her beat me. That gold medal of hers has given me all the incentive I need to get back to training again as soon as possible.'

In December 2005, Debbie married Adrian. Many of her friends and admirers from around the world, including the Steyskal family from Germany whom she had first met as a student, converged on Nassau to help the couple celebrate. Kirsten Steyskal, one of the daughters, was a bridesmaid.

Debbie looked ahead to the next Olympics, in 2008, to be held in Beijing, and hoped that she would fulfil her desire to make it four medals in four Olympics. She would also make the most of every opportunity to inspire those less fortunate and those in need of a word of encouragement to boost low self-esteem.

She had now surpassed Pauline Davis as the Queen of Bahamian track and field, enjoying a popularity unmatched among the country's sporting heroes and heroines. More importantly, she approaches every new day and challenge positively and optimistically, believing she can make a difference in the lives of the people, young and old, that she meets.

CHAPTER 7
2006–2013: A BRIEF LOOK

It is seven years since this book was first completed, a long time in the life of a top athlete. If readers look back over the first seven years of Debbie's career, they will remark on the number of significant events that occurred during that time. In the seven years up to 2013, Debbie remained a high-profile figure in the world of women's track and field and travelled the globe, competing at the top. During the first seven years, however, she was experiencing events and happenings for the first time; latterly, as her professional career has extended, the annual meets in Europe became more familiar territory for her, along with the Olympic Games and biennial World Championships. Her achievements at these events have cemented her place in the history of women's sprinting worldwide and enabled her to emerge as the most decorated and most highly appreciated athlete in The Bahamas.

Debbie did not hang up her spikes in 2008 after the Beijing Olympics, as she had first suggested. She was tempted, but, after rising to the occasion in typical but nonetheless spectacular fashion in China, she yearned for another tilt at a medal, so decided to delay her retirement until after the World Championships in Berlin in 2009. There she was on top form, made the finals of both the 100 and the 200 metres, winning a bronze medal in the longer race, and then anchoring the 4×100-metre relay team to a silver in the final.

After such an outstanding championship, it was inconceivable for her to retire: she still believed that she had it in her to 'win the big one'. She pointed to her record of finals appearances in major championships as evidence that her self-belief was based on more than confidence in her own ability and faith in her knack of rising to the big occasions.

In 2013 she was still competing. There were ups and downs, as her body would find the constant training, travelling and competing more difficult. Certainly, in recent years, she has not been so consistent or so successful. Injuries had begun to plague her and reduced both her appearances on the world stage and her chances of success in the most prestigious events.

Such was her reputation and personality, however, that she remained in high demand on the circuit; and whenever the big events came around, she was always on top of the list of Bahamian athletes for foreign sports journalists. Brent Stubbs, *Tribune* sports editor, would always be asked about her chances before any other Bahamian athlete, and the questions always focused on her chances of a medal.

Much of this is due to her honesty, realism and grace in interviews. 'Win or lose,' said Stubbs, 'Debbie is willing to sit and explain, project and congratulate others. She never lets the press down and always provides good copy.'

2006: coming back from surgery

After the two surgeries in 2005, Debbie spent much of 2006 recuperating. She was fit and strong enough to win both the 100- and the 200-metre finals in the national championships in Nassau, but she did not go to Melbourne for the Commonwealth Games with The Bahamas team, so did not defend the titles won in Manchester in 2002.

2007: promoted to gold

In 2007, Debbie began to concentrate more on the 200 metres, considered by most track and field experts as her better event. She did not enter the 100 metres in the nationals in Nassau, but easily claimed the 200-metre crown. A little later that year, she went with The Bahamas team to Osaka, Japan, for the World Championships. Although she had not been focusing on the shorter sprint, she still qualified, and in the 200 metres, but Osaka was not a memorable competition. She made the semi-finals in both races, but was far from her best and did not make either final. She was happy for her training partner, Lauryn Williams, who placed second in the 100-metre final, clocking the same time as the winner, Jamaica's Veronica Campbell-Brown, separated only by the narrowest of margins shown on the photo finish. Unfortunately, the team did not qualify for the 4×100-metre relay.

An interesting twist occurred in November of that year, following a confession from Marion Jones that she had in fact used banned performance-enhancing drugs at the 2001 World Championships in Edmonton. The International Association of Athletics Federations stripped Jones of her medals and all her records and instated Debbie as the winner of the 200 metres at those championships. Although not in a packed stadium with the Bahamian national anthem playing, Debbie was presented with the gold medal, to place alongside her Olympic gold from Sydney and the other gleaming trophies on her shelves.

Debbie was very happy to receive the gold, no matter how late, and was not too critical of Jones and her cheating. 'We [the other clean athletes] all knew something was not right about her; this at least proves we were right,' was all she would say.

2008: Beijing Olympics

In 2008, the Olympic Games took place in Beijing. Debbie had been to the Far East before, but never to the People's Republic of China, and she savoured the opportunity, having lost none of her love of travelling and experiencing new places. Debbie was again selected unanimously by the coaches, administrators and her teammates to carry the Bahamian flag at the opening ceremony. She had been so honoured in Athens and was no less proud second time around. It is extremely unusual for athletes from countries with large contingents to carry their flag more than once. Certainly no one from The Bahamas has ever done so.

She was still concentrating on the 200 metres, but had qualified for the 100 metres as well, so was entered for both distances. Furthermore, it must be added, she enjoyed an outstanding Olympics, running two series of races in the 100 and 200 metres that any female sprinter would be proud to call her own.

In the shorter distance there were four rounds. Debbie's record was: round 1 – second in heat in 11.17 seconds; round 2 – first in heat in 11.21 seconds; semi-final – fourth in 11.22 seconds; final – seventh in 11.19. Four high-powered, top-level races over two days, and a difference of just 0.05 seconds between her fastest and slowest times: proof, if any were needed, of her consistency and her competitive spirit. In the final, the three Jamaicans were led home by Shelly-Ann Fraser-Pryce to take the top three places, with Debbie's training partner, Lauryn Williams, coming in fourth.

In the 200 metres, Debbie again ran magnificently, especially in the second round, when the draw placed her in the same heat as gold medallists Veronica Campbell-Brown and Allyson Felix. Calling on all her reserves of strength and her focus, a third place won her a place in the semi-final, and from there she progressed to take her place in the final. She ran an excellent time, 22.61, but the rigours and demands of five consecutive days of intense sprinting had taken their toll, and she had to be content with seventh place, 0.8 seconds behind Veronica Campbell-Brown.

There might not have been any medals, but Debbie had nonetheless achieved a unique milestone. By reaching the finals of both sprints, she became the first woman in history to make the finals in the 100 and the 200 metres in three Olympic Games. Debbie was understandably proud to have maintained such a magnificent standard and achieved such a record, claiming a place in the top eight female sprinters in the world from 2000 to 2008.

After the Olympics, Debbie returned to The Bahamas, rested and then stepped back onto the treadmill of training in Miami with her coach, Amy Deem. But the atmosphere no longer seemed right. Training with Lauryn Williams and Coach Deem had ceased to be refreshing and rejuvenating. Debbie persevered until April 2009, but when she returned from the Penn Relay competition, she knew something had to be done. She had already been talking to her good friend, Veronica Campbell-Brown, about her coach, Lance Brauman, who worked in Orlando. At the end of April, Debbie left the familiar surroundings of the University of Miami and Coach Deem and flew to Orlando to join Brauman, Veronica Campbell-Brown and another top sprinter, American Tyson Gay.

The move proved invigorating and provided a new impetus, both physical and mental. The new regimen inspired Debbie and she approached the 2009 season with her hopes high. 'I had become unhappy where I was,' she reasons, 'and I knew I had to make the move. I think it's the best decision I could have made.'

2009: World Championships, Berlin

Early in 2009, Debbie set the world's fastest time for the 200 metres – a time that was bettered that season only by the great Allyson Felix – and easily won both sprints at The Bahamas National Championships in June. Her target, however, was the World Championships in Berlin in August. Still focusing more strongly on the longer sprint, Debbie nevertheless qualified for the 100 metres as well and enjoyed herself unreservedly, posting one of her best times – 11.05 seconds – in the final, where she placed sixth, just pipping fellow Golden Girl Chandra Sturrup, who was credited with the same time.

The 200 metres again brought out the very best in Debbie, who stormed to the final by winning her semi in 22.24 seconds. Lining up against perennial opponents Veronica Campbell-Brown and Allyson Felix, Debbie gave it all she possessed and finished third, just six-hundredths of a second behind her new training partner. Debbie was overjoyed at gaining another medal – the bronze – in a World Championships.

The celebrations did not end there. The Bahamas women entered the 4×100-metre relay in confident mood and proceeded to realise everyone's expectations. In addition to Debbie were Golden Girl Chandra Sturrup, Christine Amertil and Sheniqua Ferguson. In the heat they came in behind Jamaica, and then stood and watched as their next most dangerous rival, the US, dropped the baton and did not finish in their heat. 'That gave us a great boost,' says Debbie. 'Not wanting to gloat, of course, but the US missing the final definitely improved our chances of a medal.'

The Bahamians seized their chance and chased strongly around the track, on the shoulder of the Jamaicans. At the finish, the Jamaicans claimed the gold by just two-tenths of a second from Debbie, who anchored The Bahamas team to a well-deserved silver. Speaking about the relay, Debbie enthused, 'We knew we had a chance of medalling and we did all we could to get it. Everything clicked in the final and we were so close to upsetting the Jamaican team. I'm very happy for my teammates and for the country. It was a great team effort.'

Interestingly, after her impressive performances in Berlin, Debbie made a surprising decision, to delay retirement again and keep competing for at least another three years, focusing this time on the London Olympics in 2012 as her swansong.

2010: the Diamond League and a Circle of Honor

After such an outstanding year in 2009, an anticlimax was always likely, and 2010 proved to be just that. It was a season of niggling injuries that kept Debbie from competing in many of the events in which she wanted to take part. She even missed the National Championships in Nassau, so was not eligible for the team for the Commonwealth Games in Delhi.

There were, however, two highlights: one was a second place finish in the Diamond League meet in London in August. The Diamond League series had replaced the Eurocentric Golden League and aimed to enhance the worldwide appeal of athletics by staging events outside Europe. Athletes from all five continents compete in a series of races around the world and accumulate points depending on their finishing place. The athletes with the highest number of points receive a substantial cash prize. Debbie had missed too many events through the season to have any chance of winning the cash prize for the 200 metres, but the one-off success in London did much to redeem an unspectacular year on the track.

The second highlight was induction into the University of Georgia's Circle of Honor, its highest sporting tribute, reserved for only the most outstanding athletes who have graced the Bulldogs' playing fields. Speaking about the honour, Debbie said, 'I am really thankful for the award. It is very impressive to have my name etched in history. Whenever I step on the track I know I am representing UGA and The Bahamas.'

In 2011, Debbie continued to focus on the 200 metres, with occasional forays into the 100 metres as diversions from the serious racing. It did not hinder her from winning both events at The Bahamas National Championships for the second time in three years, and it demonstrated strongly that, even at 35 and among a growing number of young challengers, there was not only plenty of life in her legs, but also that she was determined not to relinquish her position as national champion without a fight.

2011: World Championships, Daegu

The National Championships were used to select the team for the World Championships in Daegu, South Korea. Debbie decided that she would compete only in the 200 metres and the 4×100-metre relay.

South Korea was familiar ground from the World Student Games in 1993. Debbie prepared meticulously and produced another set of outstanding sprints, to reach the final of the 200 metres. Unfortunately, she did not rise to the occasion in the final and had to be content with sixth place in 22.91 seconds, her slowest time in the championships.

Having done so well in the relay in Berlin two years earlier, The Bahamas women were confident of posing a real threat to close rivals Jamaica and the United States, but no one could have foreseen what was to befall the team in the heats. All began well, with Sheniqua Ferguson, who had grown in confidence and stature since Berlin, leading off with a very fine first leg. She handed over to newcomer Nivea Smith, who ran as if her life depended on it and reached the hand-off in second place. Anthonique Strachan (one of the new breed of female sprinters The Bahamas has been producing steadily over the last five years, and then World Junior Champion) set off and Nivea handed her the baton. Anthonique stretched her legs to go, but suddenly the two Bahamian girls tripped each other and lay tangled and sprawling on the Daegu track. Debbie could only look on in dismay. Anthonique, to her immense credit, got up and tried to catch the other runners. She blazed around the curve, but was already too far behind. She eventually reached Debbie, who chased down the home stretch, but there was too much distance to make up and the team finished sixth, nine seconds behind the US winners.

All the girls were disappointed. Debbie was philosophical, remarking that little accidents like this go to show how narrow the line is between success and failure. She knew, after years of experience, that if something similar had happened in Sydney 11 years before, her whole history might have been completely different.

2012

Early in 2012, The Bahamas unveiled its new National Stadium, funded and built by the Chinese. As part of the opening ceremony, Savatheda, Chandra, Pauline and Debbie re-enacted their gold medal relay run from the 2000 Sydney Olympics.

With the London Olympics as its climax, Debbie looked forward to 2012 with genuine optimism. When she returned to Florida in

January to begin preparing for the season with Coach Brauman, she was relaxed and self-assured, with an inner belief that she had the ability to present a serious challenge for medals. At first, training went well, but a niggling, and sometimes acute, pain in her heel and ankle started to trouble her. She tried to ignore it and concentrate on speed and technique, but she could not totally forget it.

She went to Jamaica in early May and competed in a 100-metre race, but finished in pain and was forced to rest and miss a number of important meets in Europe. She had to forego the individual events in The Bahamas National Championships. Fortunately, she had already made the Olympic qualifying times in both the 100 and the 200 metres, but faced a conundrum regarding the 4×100-metre relay.

The International Olympic Committee has strict regulations relating to the relays: only the 16 fastest national teams are allowed to compete. In early June, The Bahamas was outside the top 16 and knew that without Debbie they had only a minimal chance of qualifying. She had run through the pain in Brazil in May with the team, but they had not met as a team since.

To everybody's surprise, Debbie arrived in Nassau two weeks prior to the Nationals and announced that she was prepared to run in the relay with the other team members at the Silver Lightning Athletic Club's meet. A special relay event with a couple of other national teams was being staged for the girls to try to reach a time fast enough to reach the top 16. 'I'm prepared to give it a go and do whatever I can to help The Bahamas qualify,' Debbie stated before the race.

She taped up the ankle, took some painkillers and joined Sheniqua Ferguson, Chandra Sturrup and Anthonique Strachan in this crucial race.

'This is no time to think about injury,' pledged Debbie. 'The Bahamas is in danger of not qualifying, so I have to do whatever

I can to help. Mentally, I feel I can do it, but there is still some pain.' In fact, there was a sharp pain every time her foot struck the ground: her injury had been diagnosed as a severe bone bruise. Deciding to run for the benefit of the team in this way offers yet another example of her relentless determination and loyalty to her teammates and country.

The other members of the team were very pleased with the decision. They were relieved too, because they knew she could make the difference between qualifying and not qualifying for London. Sheniqua and Anthonique were in very good form, and Chandra was approaching her best once again after some troublesome injuries. 'Q (Sheniqua) and Anthonique are running well,' said Debbie, 'and we have a great shot to qualify. I'm just ready to work through the pain to help. The team needs me so I have to be available to help.'

Selflessly, Debbie was prepared to assist the team, even if it meant suppressing her aspirations for an individual medal. 'This is my last Olympics,' she reasoned, 'so I just want to go out there and represent my country well. If I make my injury worse and have to take the rest of the year off, then so be it. At least I'll know that I did my job and helped us qualify for the Olympics. I can't guarantee that I will be healthy for the Olympics, but I know that together we can do it.'

There was a premonition in those last words: even with a prolonged rest from mid-June to August, she was just a shadow of herself on the track in London. Her efforts had indeed helped the team to qualify, but they had also caused the injury to worsen and set back her recovery. She could not summon sufficient speed in either the 100 or the 200, and for the first time in her life, the only woman to have reached double finals in three successive Olympic Games failed to qualify for the semi-finals.

When the relay heats came round, the coaches left her out of the team, much to her annoyance. Despite running a season's best, the girls, with Christine Amertil in place of Debbie, failed to reach the final by 0.33 seconds.

Debbie could not understand why she had been overlooked, because none of the coaches had even spoken to her before the race. She assumed they thought her foot was too much of a problem, but it added to the irritation she felt towards the coaches and administrators in London.

Debbie has always been outspoken and said what she believes, but she rarely criticises in public. After London, however, she spoke passionately about the lack of communication between coaches and athletes, saying that none of the coaches spoke to her at all during the games. She bemoaned the lack of a full team meeting when the team arrived in London, although such meetings help to build team spirit and cohesiveness among the members, which can have a positive influence on performance. She was also unhappy with the team uniforms, which were not new and somewhat shabby, she felt. Without the gold medal performance by the men's 4×400-metre relay team, she concluded, beating the US, London 2012 would have been a miserable Olympics for her.

Sadly, pain in her heel and ankle meant that she had to rest for the remainder of 2012. The year ended with another sad loss: Tommy Robinson, an important father figure and mentor in her early life, lost his long battle with cancer in December 2012. Debbie was in Nassau for the funeral, and for once her spirit seemed clouded and her bubbly spirit flattened. She was very distressed by Tommy's passing and made no attempt to hide her emotions. She was consoled, however, by the fact that the new stadium, like the old one, would carry Tommy's name – the Thomas A. Robinson National Stadium.

2013

As 2013 unfolded, it was unclear whether Debbie would be fit for the World Championships in Moscow. Off the track, however, she remained as busy and involved as ever. She returned to assist at McDonald's outlets on World Children's Day every November and will continue to do so. 'Our children are the future of our country,' she says. 'I could not be happier to do all that I can to ensure that every Bahamian child receives the same chance in life as everyone else. I've been so glad to partner with McDonald's for the last seven years and am proud to be their World Children's Day spokesperson for The Bahamas.'

She had her tenure extended as athlete representative on the IAAF and she remains an ambassador for the United Nations Food and Agriculture Organization.

More importantly, she continues to be an inspiration and a role model for all athletes in The Bahamas. Brent Stubbs, *Tribune* Sports Editor, believes that she is the greatest Bahamian athlete of all time, given her achievements, her longevity and her personality. Stubbs reckons that the only Bahamian athlete who even approaches Debbie is doubles tennis player Mark Knowles (ranked number 1 doubles player in the world at the turn of the century and holder of three Grand Slam doubles titles).

In 2013, Debbie was on the verge of passing on the mantle of sprint queen to a successor. She could see great potential in two girls: Anthonique Strachan, who had already cemented her place in the one-lap relay team, and Shaunae Miller, champion at the 100, 200 and 400 metres.

'Anthonique has surpassed me at CARIFTA,' said Debbie, 'by winning the Austin Sealy award twice, and she is also a World Junior Champion. Shaunae is incredible. She won the Austin Sealy at this year's CARIFTA and I call her The Bahamas' Usain Bolt. Her potential is without limit – and she's now a Georgia Bulldog too!'

There were others coming through about whom Debbie was very enthusiastic, impressed by their dedication, but also their humility. It seems that her influence goes beyond just the running and has affected and moulded character and personality too.

In 2013, retirement beckoned. Debbie vowed to give up after Moscow that summer, and move on to coaching at a US college once she had gained her coaching qualifications. Might she be tempted to push back retirement even further? We remember that one of her heroines, Merlene Ottey, the great Jamaican sprinter, went to six Olympic Games and, in 2012, at the age of 52, anchored Slovenia's 4×100-metre relay team in the European Championships. (Ottey had married a Slovenian and became a Slovenian citizen.)

In another scenario, if her injury and lack of training meant having to miss the Moscow Worlds in 2013, would Debbie want to return to Beijing for the World Championships in 2015, and retire after performing there?

Time alone will answer that question. We remain with the certainty that the greatest Bahamian athlete of all time, who rose from the humblest of beginnings, has given thousands of Bahamians great pleasure and joy over 17 years of top-class, world-beating sprinting. We also know that she will continue to do her best for her country and 'her endeavour best' to resist the challenge to her domestic crowns from the new breed of younger female sprinters, as long as there is strength in her legs and breath in her body.